RE-AUTHORING
LIVES

Carl Bley

OCTOBER,
1995

RE-AUTHORING LIVES:
INTERVIEWS
& ESSAYS

by

Michael White

DULWICH CENTRE PUBLICATIONS
Adelaide, South Australia

CONTENTS

Introduction

This collection brings together six interviews and three essays. Of the interviews, four have appeared in various journals in recent years. About these I will not say much here. In making my decision about what to include in this collection, I did review these pieces, and quickly concluded that, with the benefit of hindsight, I would now put differently a number of points that I raised in them. I was tempted to footnote them with clarifications, provisos, and revisions. However, after some deliberation, I decided that the continuities in the thought and practice that are reflected in these pieces and in my present position on matters of my work and my life far outweigh the discontinuities, so I decided to let these stand as they were.

The two previously unpublished interviews that I have chosen for inclusion in this collection are entitled: *Psychotic experience and discourse*, and *Naming abuse and breaking from its effects*. The foundation for the first of these was put down in 1990, when Ken Stewart interviewed me about a range of subjects that were mostly related to contemporary processes of "normalising judgement", and to the common and taken-for-granted practices of subjugation in the "mental health" field. We decided to revise this interview, and this provided me with an opportunity to reflect more extensively on my thoughts about these issues, and to give an account of some of my work with people who have psychiatric diagnoses - chiefly schizophrenia - and who are considered to be "chronically ill". This is an opportunity that I have greatly appreciated, for, although I have represented these thoughts and practices in my teaching for some years, I have not previously managed to organise myself to bring them together in a publishable form.

After reviewing *Psychotic experience and discourse* for the purposes of this collection, I am not at all sure that I have succeeded in providing an adequate sense of what this work has meant to me personally, or that I have emphasised enough the part that the creation and the acknowledgement of "community" has had to play in this work. For the personal part, I find the steps that people take in revising their relationship with their psychotic experience, and in challenging assigned ways of life, to be inspiring - how could it be otherwise? But, ahead of this, I find that my life is deeply touched by the faith expressed by these people, a faith that is reflected in their tireless efforts to search out and enter into yet further consultations about their lives. Although the nature of these efforts usually goes unrecognised, when these people's experience of the landscape of the culture of psychotherapy has been so relentlessly barren, this is a faith that I can only experience as tenacious.

For the community part, I am not just referring to the importance of those legitimate and acknowledged networks that are initiated by community mental health projects, but also to those "illegitimate" and mostly unrecognised networks that these people go about building for themselves with others whom they strongly identify with - those others who are considered marginal, those who, in Goffman's terms, have experienced "spoiled identities". An example: I was recently consulted by a solemn young man who talked of his "psychiatric history", and who, midway through the consultation, presented me with a rather grimy and slightly tattered letter. As I read this document aloud, the young man started to cry. I recognised the content of the letter. This was a "document of identity" that I had assisted another young man, whom I will call James, also with a "psychiatric history", to put together some eighteen months previously - only the name and the signature at the bottom had been changed. The young man and I talked about how he had come by the document, his identification with it, the circumstances under which James had encouraged him to substitute his own name, the generosity of this gesture, and about what this had meant to him. I then understood that this young man was crying for himself, and that these were tears of compassion, tears of a sort that, until this time, he had never been able to spill on his own behalf. And I learned from this young man that, in expressing this, he experienced James and many other young people crying with him, and that this provided a sense of community that was sustaining of him. Together, and with some joy, we began to plan some steps that we thought might bring acknowledgement to those people in this "other" support network for the contributions that they were making to each other's lives.

Naming abuse and breaking from its effects also brings together some thoughts and practices that I have been sharing with others in different teaching contexts over some years. I am grateful to Chris McLean for the background work that he undertook for the purpose of preparing himself for this interview, particularly as I experience a significant degree of relief in seeing this piece published. I say relief, because I have been deeply regretful over not having worked these thoughts and practices into a publishable form at an earlier date. This is a delay that I regard as unfortunate.

Therapeutic interaction is a two-way phenomenon. We get together with people for a period of time over a range of issues, and all of our lives are changed for this. On some occasions these therapeutic interactions change our lives more significantly than on other occasions. When we are consulted by people who have survived abuse, and who are challenging the effects of this abuse in their lives, we are personally confronted to challenge much of what we have felt bound by in our own lives. Those people who are determined to break from the effects of various abuses that they have been subject to demonstrate a radical responsibility for the choices that they make about the discontinuities and the continuities of their lives. These choices about discontinuities are witnessed in their refusal to visit on others the abuses that have been visited on them, and in their determination to dispossess those who have perpetrated the abuse of the "last say" in matters of personal identity. These choices about continuities are witnessed in their life-long determination to keep alive those precious sparks of hope - the hope that things might be different at some future time - despite the absolute discouragement of this, and in their maintenance of a fierce allegiance to whatever it is that has seen them through the dark hours of their lives.

In being privy to the performance of this radical responsibility for one's choices in life, we cannot be so resigned to the "received" versions of our own lives. We are personally confronted with a whole range of choices about the continuities and the discontinuities of our own lives, and by the responsibility that we have to honour the invitation that these people are extending to us - to walk with them and to join them in making it our business to expose and to challenge the injustices of our world in whatever situations we find ourselves.

In addition to the interviews, I have included three essays in this collection. *Therapeutic documents revisited* addresses a couple of the frequently stated concerns: about the economics of engaging in these practices of the written word, and about the significance of these practices to people who consult therapists. *Behaviour and its determinants, or action and its sense: Systems and narrative metaphors*, is a short piece that I wrote about eighteen months ago in response to what I perceived to be, at that time, a general lack of rigour in thought in our field. *Reflecting teamwork as definitional ceremony* provides an account of certain practices of reflecting team work that are informed by the narrative metaphor and by a critical perspective, and which in some respects mirror some of the processes of Barbara Myerhoff's "definitional ceremonies". These are reflecting team practices that provide all parties to the therapeutic interaction with significant opportunities for what Myerhoff might define as the "re-membering" of their lives.

On reviewing these pieces together, I become aware of just how much acknowledging there is to be done. So let me begin this. In a number of the pieces that make up this collection, readers will find a focus on the politics of gender. On many occasions over the years that I have been presenting this work, others have referred to me as a "pro-feminist man". I have always experienced discomfort with this definition of my identity, and have always protested it on several counts. Because men do not have women's experience of the world, I don't believe that men can be pro-feminist by identity. I am for pro-feminist action, but what sort of men's actions are in the interests of women can only be decided upon by women. I am concerned that for men to propose or to accede to a pro-feminist identity is likely to marginalise this consideration - that, under these circumstances, there is a very significant risk that, in judging their actions, men will place faith in their individual consciousness, and cease to actively solicit women's feedback about what is in their interests, and to give this feedback primacy.

I also have difficulty with the notion of a pro-feminist identity because this obscures my own personal stake in any of the actions that I take to challenge men's domination of others. Growing up in men's culture, I have been on the receiving end of men's excesses and abuses of power. And, for a good part of my life, I witnessed, with great heartache, such abuses being inflicted on those whom I love. So, in the actions that I am engaged in to address local injustices, many of which are related to the politics of gender, I am addressing this heartache. It is not just for women that I make it my business to do this - it is for me as well.

So, what does this have to do with acknowledgement? I don't think that it is possible for men to venture very far outside of the dominant men's culture, even if they experience alienation from it, without assistance from women. And, as I have already said, pro-feminist action cannot be a matter of men's individual consciousness. The attention that I give in my work to the politics of gender is an outcome of the conversations that I've had with women who have a feminist politics, and who have been prepared to raise the difficult issues, not so much in regard to the practices of therapy specifically, but in regard to relationships between men and women more generally - women who have been prepared to "put themselves on the line", in the company of men, in their frank expressions of their experience of these relationships. And, in regard to this, and much, much more, I would particularly like to acknowledge the conversations that Cheryl White and I have shared through the history of our connection. These have been conversations in the context of a partnership in which Cheryl has constantly questioned the limits on what I have been able to think in regard to gender, and, for that matter, culture and race. I have experienced this partnership as a fount of generativity.

Then there is the contribution of all those people who have sought consultations over many years. In countless ways, they have been a source of ongoing renewal in this work, and their feedback, generously given, has assisted me to distinguish between ideas that are helpful and ideas that are unhelpful. There is the support, the enthusiasm, the goodwill and, of course, the questions and the comments, of all those therapists who have attended training events here in Adelaide and elsewhere, and who have contributed in many ways to the definition of this work. There are friends and colleagues to thank for their encouragement. I won't begin to name these people here, because I don't know where I would end this, or even if I could. I will make one special mention - David Epston, my close friend and colleague, who, for some time, has been encouraging me to put together this collection. In my connection with David, I have always found a camaraderie, one that has been a source of personal fortitude and that has provided me with a sense of solidarity in this work, which has been essential to me in carrying this work forward into unfamiliar and, at times, unwelcoming contexts.

Finally, I would like to express my appreciation to those who initiated the interviews that form the significant body of this collection: Donald Bubenzer, John West, Shelly Boughner, Lesley Allen, Andrew Wood, Christopher McLean and Ken Stewart. These people achieved a great deal through the careful preparations that they undertook for these interviews - they managed to address just so many of the important questions and the salient issues.

1. The Narrative Perspective in Therapy *

Interviewers: ** *Donald L. Bubenzer*
John D. West
Shelly R. Boughner

INFLUENCES ON THERAPEUTIC APPROACH

Donald: Why don't we start, Michael, by sharing some of the ideas and theories that have influenced your professional life.

Michael: In terms of theories, early in my career I was interested in following up some of the schools of family therapy. Toward the end of the seventies, I got more interested in looking at some of the ideas that informed the schools of family therapy. I decided to go back and make my own interpretation of those ideas, rather than just accept the interpretations of the originators of these schools. I started doing this at the end of the seventies, and became particularly interested in the work of Gregory Bateson. I recall feeling quite excited about the possibilities associated with

* Reprinted, with permission, from "The Family Journal: Counseling and therapy for couples and families", 1994, 2(1):71-83. ©ACA. No further reproduction authorised without written permission of the American Counseling Association.

** Donald L. Bubenzer and John D. West are faculty members, and Shelly R. Boughner a doctoral candidate, in the Counseling and Human Development Services Program at the Kent State University, Kent, Ohio. They can be contacted at 310 White Hall, Kent State University, Kent, Oh. 44242, USA. (This interview was conducted in Atlanta, March 1993.)

interpreting these ideas myself, and exploring the implications of these interpretations in practice with families. Also, earlier in the 1970s, I had become interested in the philosophy of science, with a particular focus on the phenomenon of scientific revolution in the scientific community. This led me into looking at how certain paradigms are, if you like, thrown over and replaced with others - this work is really about radical transformation in social systems. Of the many ideas that have caught my attention through the eighties, those of Michel Foucault (1973, 1979, 1980, 1984), a French intellectual, have been most influential. I guess I've always been more interested in reading outside the boundaries of the profession, rather than inside. Feminist theory has been very important, and I've drawn fairly heavily from literary theory, anthropology, critical theory, and so on - in fact from many domains that have contributed to the explication and exploration of the more recent developments in social theory.

Donald: It seems like almost all of the practitioners and theorists we've talked with have indicated that their inspiration comes from outside the discipline or theory. What are your thoughts on how this outside perspective encourages new ideas?

Michael: I think that reading outside the discipline is more likely to provide us with metaphors that encourage new ways of thinking about therapy. And I think such reading, particularly when it relates to the more recent developments in social theory, including critical theory, also helps us to consider the various ways that we are, or might be, reproducing dominant culture within the therapeutic discipline. This also assists us to consider how various aspects of this cultural reproduction might not be so helpful to those persons who seek our help and, for that matter, to our own lives. So, although I think there are some really sparkling things being said within the discipline, and would encourage therapists to stay abreast of the relevant reading, I do think it's really helpful to utilise ideas from the outside in that some of these ideas enable us to more critically reflect on the so-called discipline of family therapy itself. Here, I don't mean critical in a negative sense, but in a way that allows us to be more in touch with our taken-for-granted practices and ways of thinking about life and of therapy. Critical thought encourages us to review our assumptions, and to render visible some of our everyday taken-for-granted practices of life and of relationships. One outcome of this is that we become more aware of the effects of these ways of thinking and acting, and a second is that it becomes more possible for us to take responsibility for the real effects of our work on the lives of those persons who seek our help.

Donald: So where did this idea of story come into being for you?

Michael: I was initially introduced to the idea by the work of Gregory Bateson. But it was Cheryl White and David Epston who encouraged me to interpret my work according to the narrative metaphor, and to undertake a more specific exploration of this metaphor. So, I became very interested in the structure of texts.

THOUGHT UNDERLYING THE NARRATIVE PERSPECTIVE

Donald: Please explain for readers, what you mean by story or narrative as life, as being the basis of your work.

Michael: This is to propose that human beings are interpreting beings - that we are active in the interpretation of our experiences as we live our lives. It's to propose that it's not possible for us to interpret our experience without access to some frame of intelligibility, one that provides a context for our experience, one that makes the attribution of meaning possible. It's to propose that stories constitute this frame of intelligibility. It's to propose that the meanings derived in this process of interpretation are not neutral in their effects on our lives, but have real effects on what we do, on the steps that we take in life. It's to propose that it is the story or self-narrative that determines which aspects of our lived experience get expressed, and it is to propose that it is the story of self-narrative that determines the shape of the expression of our lived experience. It's to propose that we live by the stories that we have about our lives, that these stories actually shape our lives, constitute our lives, and that they "embrace" our lives.

Many people mistake the narrative proposal to be a form of representationalism. Some assume that, when I'm invoking the narrative metaphor, I'm talking about a description of life rather than about the structure of life itself; they assume that I'm suggesting that the story is a mirror of life, a reflection of life as lived - a map of the "territory" of life. And some assume that I'm proposing some sort of perspectival notion - that a specific story of life presents us with just one of many equally valid perspectives on life, so that if persons relate painful experiences, all we need to do is to encourage them to enter into a different perspective on their lives and to tell a different story. These are *representationalist assumptions* that are based on the tradition of foundationalist thought, not on the constructionist orientation that accompanies the narrative metaphor.

If we assume that our lives are constituted through narrative, it really is not possible for us to take the position that "one story is as good as another". Moral relativism is ruled out. Instead, we will be making it our business to attend to the real effects of those stories that constitute persons' lives.

Donald: Is there an underlying value system by which you evaluate the relative worth of the stories?

Michael: Yes, always. But not a system of values that has an allegiance to established norms or so-called "universals".

Donald: And so, it's a kind of a constructionist perspective, within the context of an underlying value system.

Michael: I don't think that there is any constructionist position that can escape a confrontation with questions of values and personal ethics. In fact, according to my understanding, the constructionist position emphasises these questions, and elevates this confrontation. So, the idea that constructionist positions lead to a state of moral relativism - where there's no basis for making decisions about different actions - doesn't fit with what I know of this position. If we acknowledge that it is the stories that have been negotiated about our lives that make up or shape or constitute our lives, and if in therapy we collaborate with persons in the further negotiation or renegotiation of the stories of persons' lives, then we really are in a position of having to face and to accept, more than ever, a responsibility for the real effects of our interactions on the lives of others. We are confronted with a degree of responsibility in the assessment of the real effects of altered or alternative self-narratives.

Shelly: When you talk about the stories shaping our lives, it reminds me of the notion that "the story lives us". What is your perspective on that?

Michael: This idea about stories living us is a significant part of the equation. However, in making the point that our lives are embraced by the private but constructed stories that we have about life, I've perhaps been a little too emphatic. If the idea that stories "live us" or "embrace our lives" leads to the notion that persons go about life rather mindlessly re-enacting or reproducing these stories, then I think that it is a problematic idea. Stories provide the frames that make it possible for us to interpret our experience, and these acts of interpretation are achievements that we take an active part in. Also, a single story cannot live us in any complete sense because there isn't any single story of life that is free of ambiguity and contradiction, and that can handle all of the contingencies in life. These ambiguities, contradictions and contingencies stretch our meaning-making resources. We really work hard to resolve or make sense out of these contradictions and ambiguities, and of our experience of these contingencies - to make sense out of significant experiences that cannot be so readily interpreted through the dominant stories that we have about our lives, to make meaning out of experiences that threaten to leave us flummoxed or confused or puzzled. In this process we often elevate or invoke some of the sub-stories of our lives, and it is this multi-storied nature of life that requires at least a degree of active mediation on our behalf.

THE NARRATIVE PERSPECTIVE IN COUNSELLING/THERAPY

Donald: What are your assumptions about what constitutes human problems when people come for counselling?

Michael: When persons come along to counselling, I assume that their ways of being and thinking, or the ways of being and thinking of others, are somehow problematic for them - that the real effects of these ways of being and of thinking are experienced as negative. Some persons are more able to articulate their experience of these ways of being and thinking than others. For example, some persons make clear statements about the experiences of life that they find subjugating or disqualifying of their own preferred ways of being and of thinking.

Donald: Could you talk, for a moment, about "culture as story", and how that also relates to problems that people may experience in life?

Michael: There is a dominant story about what it means to be a person of moral worth in our culture. This is a story that emphasises self-possession, self-containment, self-actualisation, and so on. From the position that we've been discussing here, these notions are seen to be specifying or prescribing of a way of being and of thinking that shapes what is often referred to as "individuality". This individuality is a way of being that is actually a culturally preferred way of being. So, for us, the notions that accompany this dominant story about what it means to be a person of moral worth in our culture don't represent some authentic way of living, or some real or genuine expression of human nature but, rather, are really a specification or prescription of cultural preferences. We can't talk about self-possession or self-actualisation without giving a description or telling a story of what a life would look like if it were self-actualised or self-possessed. And these very descriptions or stories of what a life might look like if it were "right" are shaping of life. And what is "right" is culture-specific. What's "right" requires certain operations on our lives, much of which are gender and class-specific. Through these operations, we govern our thoughts, our relationships with others, our relationship with ourselves, even our relationship with our own bodies - our gestures, the very arrangement of our bodies in space, even how we sit and move, and so on. This is all in the service of reproducing the "privileged form" or dominant way of being of a culture.

Donald: Diversity is one of the "buzz words" by which we describe our moment, and I've assumed that perhaps social constructionism is coming to the forefront now because it can accommodate this cultural diversity better than other paradigms. What are your thoughts about why social constructionism seems to express our world better at this time?

Michael: I hope that diversity is not just a buzz word of our moment. But I fear that it may be, and I am not at all persuaded by those arguments that propose that we are now witnessing the emergence of a "postmodern" culture. Some of these arguments are based on the presumed effects of the recent and extraordinary developments in communication technologies - that these developments expose persons to, and incite them to step into, multiple realities, and that they have the effect of shaking up all of the old "certainties" and introducing persons to alternative experiences of the self, and to diversity. But I ask you the question: Could it be that the very development of these communication technologies stands apart from ideology? I think not. Could it be that these technologies mitigate the *Bad* supremacy of dominant ideologies? I think not. A strong argument can be *news* made that the opposite is the case - that these technologies have significantly contributed to the production of a transcultural "monolithic" self. Take television: sure, through this medium we are now confronted with many other images of life - of life lived otherwise - but in the presentation of these images there is always interpretation. That is, the presentation and receipt of these images, and the meanings given to these, are mediated by dominant ideology. So I think that there is a very real risk that we are developing more of an international monoculture, and it goes without saying that this would have the effect of further reducing the margins of personal and cultural freedom. I think that Chomsky (1988)

CHOMSKY

made this point in his observations about "manufacturing consent", and I find what he has to say quite convincing.

But we do not have to be resigned to a transcultural monolithic self, or to the development of a monoculture. Lots of people, perhaps more than ever, are making it their business to challenge many of the traditional "grand designs", and there has been some success at calling these into question. For example, take the grand design of the nuclear family. It doesn't really fit with what's happening in the world - not that it ever really did fit. After all, it was basically a production of the dominant ideology of the 1930s.

I think it is increasingly apparent, to all who care to look and to listen, that there are virtually as many family forms out there as there are families, and that many significantly differing forms appear to work quite well. In some circles, there is now greater interest in exploring how alternative family forms work by actually consulting the families concerned about this. In this way, persons who are involved in families that don't comply with the requirements of the nuclear family model are less likely to experience marginalisation. And, as well, alternative knowledges of family life can be honoured and more widely shared. I believe that feminist scholars have led the way in the exploration of and the honouring of other forms of social organisation and, as therapists, I think that it is time for us to stop abdicating our responsibility, and instead play a more significant part in this - to join with them in this important work.

So, if diversity is just a buzz word, I do think that, with the assistance of what we refer to as social constructionism, we might play a considerable part in breathing life into that word. Social constructionism might be applied to this task, not just because it leads to considerations that facilitate the expression of diversity, but also because it constitutes diversity.

Donald: Returning to therapy, you have argued that there are multiple stories out there, and have proposed ways that we might try to incorporate them in our work, rather than attempting, as we have in the past, to produce a dominant cultural story that, as you said, marginalises these other forms and keeps them out of the mainstream.

Michael: I think that a number of the recent developments in our field in the areas of theory, practice, and research do challenge some of the politics that have been central to a preoccupation with the reproduction of the dominant culture in counselling/therapy. For example, there has been a general challenge to some of the practices of power that have incited persons to measure their lives, relationships, families, and so on, against some notion of how they should be, and some challenges over the extent to which therapists have gone about trying to fashion persons and relationships to fit with the "ideal" frames that support these notions. I would like to reiterate that I don't believe that it is our mission to be wholly complicit in the reproduction of the dominant culture and, at least to an extent, some of the recent developments in theory and practice do enable us to step away from that position. These developments encourage us to acknowledge and to question the politics of therapy, to reject therapy as a form of the government of persons, and to consider some of the power issues that are part of all therapeutic interactions.

Donald: What would be the criteria of successful therapy from your perspective?

Michael: I'm really interested in what persons determine to be preferred ways of living and interacting with themselves and each other. That's one of my major interests in this work. If the ways of living and thinking that persons often come into therapy with aren't working for them, for whatever reason, I'm interested in providing a context that contributes to the exploration of other ways of living and thinking. There is always a stock of alternative stories about how life might be, other versions of life as lived. I'm interested in how I might assist persons to step more into those stories that are judged, by them, to be preferred - to perform the alternative understandings or meanings that these alternative stories make possible. Of course, this is not unproblematic, and there are many institutions in our society that stand in the way of this. And at times this means joining with persons in the challenging of certain structures that make this domination possible. So, at times, this practice of therapy includes a form of political action at what we might call the local level.

Donald: How do you define the point where therapy is finished?

Michael: Well, it is certainly not just when persons have different cognitions of the world. Some persons assume that the work that I am referring to is informed by cognitive theory. This doesn't resonate with me, although I couldn't say that I am at all up on developments in cognitive theory. A very significant part of my work relates to facilitating the expression of aspects of lived experience that have previously been neglected, and to a re-expression of other experiences of life through alternative frames of intelligibility. So, inevitably, through the privileging and reliving of various aspects of experience, this work is strongly emotive. In the process of therapy, as experience structures expression, and as expression structures and restructures experience, the feeling responses of all parties to the therapeutic interaction can be very intense.

You asked about the point at which therapy is finished and, in response, I would like to emphasise the transformative nature of this work. As space is opened for family members to perform the alternative and preferred stories of their lives, and for the acknowledgement of many of the alternative claims associated with these performances, the therapist becomes increasingly decentralised in the whole process, and eventually s/he is discharged from the therapy. The discharge of the therapist generally doesn't take long to happen, and it is rarely much of a surprise when it does happen. Although the therapist has played a very significant part in the co-authorship of alternative and preferred accounts of persons' lives, s/he has also worked to ensure that those persons who seek help are the privileged co-authors in this collaboration. So, as persons go some way in the articulation and the experience of other ways of being and thinking that are available to them, as they experience some of the purposes, values, beliefs, commitments, and so on, that are associated with these alternative accounts of life, they approach a point at which the therapist's contribution is unnecessary. It makes perfect sense to discharge the therapist at this point, and this can be celebrated.

TOOLS AND TECHNIQUES OF THE NARRATIVE PERSPECTIVE

Donald: Let's move to talking about the tools and techniques involved in working from a narrative perspective. Let's explore how you get started, how change gets introduced, how it is sustained, and so forth. When you sit down with a family the first time, and are beginning to introduce the change process, what are your thoughts and what are the techniques you use?

Michael: Wow, that's a big question! [laughter] I'm really interested in people's accounts of their experience. I really want to understand what life has been like for them. So, I guess the first part of my work is to try to get some appreciation of what persons have been going through. I think it's important that I achieve a degree of understanding about this, and I think that it's important that persons are aware that I have achieved at least a degree of this understanding. So this is really quite basic, and over the years it has been said by many people in this field. However, in stating this, I am not proposing that the interaction with persons around the development of this understanding is neutral, or that the development of this understanding is neutral in its real effects on the shape of the therapy, and on persons' lives more generally. So we have to be well connected to the real effects - as these are spontaneously reported and as they are solicited by us - of our interaction with persons around the development of these understandings, and of the understandings themselves, as they evolve. We all know that there are ways of talking about our experience and ways of talking about our experience - some profoundly unhelpful, and some that raise new possibilities.

I often achieve some of this requisite understanding by exploring, with persons, their experiences of the problem. This has the effect of introducing a particular class of conversation, one that I refer to as an *externalizing conversation*. I encourage persons to provide an account of how the problem has been affecting their lives and their relationships. Often, in the early stages at least, for persons to enter this conversation necessitates something of a shift.

It is not at all unusual to find persons engaged in internalizing conversations about that which is problematic. This is largely a cultural phenomenon, one that so often reproduces the very problems that persons are attempting to resolve. So, parents might say "Johnny's the problem". In response, I'll ask questions that introduce a more externalizing conversation about that which is problematic: "How is the problem affecting Johnny's life? What is it doing to his friendships? How is it interfering in his relationships with you as parents? What do you think it is doing to how Johnny feels about himself? What is the problem doing to Johnny's picture of himself as a person? What sort of interactions is it dictating in his relationships with other people? As Johnny's parents, how does this problem effect you personally? Does it ever have you doing and saying things that go against your better judgement?" and so on. And, of course, I will ask Johnny for his opinion on the same questions. This line of questioning leads to externalizing conversations about that which is problematic.

Donald: You're saying, first, that you attempt to understand the people who come to you, and want them to know that you understand, as a way of gaining confidence between the two parties, and as a way of gathering some information, and as a way of establishing new possibilities. And then, secondly, you try to create a different atmosphere around the problem, one in which people see the problem as not being intrinsic to them, but as being something that is acting upon them from outside.

Michael: Yes. Over time, persons come to believe that the problem speaks of their identity - so often problems present persons with what they take to be certain truths about their character, nature, purposes, and so on, and these truths have a totalising effect on their lives. The externalizing conversations challenge all of this. The internalizing conversations that persons have entered into around that which is problematic for them have invariably had negative effects on their lives.

Interacting around the idea that problems are inherent to certain relationships, or intrinsic to persons' lives, generally reinforces these truths and perpetuates that which persons experience as problematic. And these internalizing conversations around that which is problematic also make it very difficult for persons to experience new possibilities for action. If you are the problem, or if your relationship is the problem, then there's not much that you can do - except maybe to act against yourself. Externalizing conversations challenge much of this. They make it possible for persons to experience an identity that is distinct or separate from the problem. Through externalizing conversations, the problem is to an extent disempowered, as it no longer speaks to persons of the truth about who they are as people, or about the very nature of their relationships. This opens new possibilities for action. In the evolution of these externalizing conversations, persons continue to revise their relationship with their problems.

Donald: I believe you've used the term *mapping the effects of the problem* to describe this part of the process.

Michael: Yes. I've talked about mapping the effects of the problem in people's lives and their relationships. This is most helpful when the problem is particularly entrenched or seems particularly intractable over a period of time. At these times, it might be appropriate that the externalizing conversation be quite extensive. Take the example of anorexia nervosa, where young women really believe that certain disciplinary ways of operating on their bodies, their thoughts, and their souls, are in the service of shaping an authentic way of being. In order for these persons to experience a degree of alienation from these ways of going about their life, in order for them to somehow experience disenchantment with the forces of anorexia nervosa, the externalizing conversations usually need to be quite extensive.

Shelly: I wonder if you've thought about it in terms of allowing hope to enter in. When people feel like the problem is all that there is and that it is the total reality, for them to just get the sense that it might be different than that, would be hope-inspiring.

Michael: People say that they experience this process as freeing, or as opening up new possibilities. So, I think it introduces a lot of hope.

Donald: Would the outcome of these externalizing conversations be what you call deconstruction?

Michael: Yes. From my perspective this would be a form of deconstruction. This form has to do with deconstructing those so-called "truths" that persons have experienced as so capturing of their lives. We can ask other questions that further this process, perhaps some that bring forth the history of certain "truths", like "How do you think you were recruited into this idea about who you are?" I believe that, although internalizing conversations obscure the politics of experience, externalizing conversations emphasise the politics of experience. And whenever the politics of experience is emphasised, there are possibilities for deconstruction.

Donald: Is deconstructing always a preface to re-storying?

Michael: If you are referring particularly to externalizing conversations, then the answer is no. Externalizing conversations seem particularly important when the problems that persons experience are quite totalising of their lives - in other words, when it seems that stories that family members have about their lives and each other are quite problem-saturated. At these times, externalizing conversations as deconstructing conversations are very helpful. However, there are many times when persons come along to therapy and it's quite clear that there are other narratives of self and relationships that are relatively available, despite being somewhat overshadowed by the more dominant accounts of their lives.

When these alternative narratives provide for persons' preferred accounts of their lives, therapy structured around them creates the opportunity for persons to step more fully into preferred ways of being, right from the outset. But this re-storying is of itself deconstructing of the dominant accounts of persons' lives - of the truths that are associated with these dominant accounts. Perhaps this is a version of deconstruction that is more in keeping with the Derridian (Derrida 1977) sense of this.

Donald: So you ask yourself how pervasive the story is in persons' lives, and how much they can focus on re-storying. If they can't focus on re-storying, that's a clue to you to focus on deconstruction through externalizing conversations.

Michael: That's right. If persons find it really difficult to give meaning to an event that contradicts the dominant story, then it's often necessary to engage in more of an externalizing conversation. However, there are many occasions when it's not that difficult to give meaning to contradiction. I might facilitate this through a series of questions like: *Hey, wait a minute. This doesn't seem to fit with these other things that you've been talking about. Tell me more about these. How did you take that step? Would you say that this is a positive development or a negative development? What do you think are the foundations for this step? As we reflect on this development, what does this tell you about how you really want things to be?* and so on. People can very often step into these conversations quite quickly, without an extended externalizing conversation.

Donald: It seems like the whole idea of deconstructing a story is something that other constructionist therapists, who are more solution-oriented, are distancing from. They're trying to focus on how to get the client to work towards a goal. Your deconstruction work seems to be an added dimension which is missing from the work of some others in this area.

Michael: I'm not sure how to respond to your question. I am not much of an authority on the intricacies of solution-oriented therapy, and certainly wouldn't be happy to refer to my work in this way. In saying this, I'm not suggesting that my work is not oriented towards solutions, and I'm not passing comment on solution-oriented therapy. In fact, I believe that the solution-oriented therapists have made a very significant contribution. But

I'm not at all satisfied that the description "solution- oriented" captures the spirit of my work. And I certainly wouldn't say that my work is primarily goal-oriented. I'm vitally interested in history. I think that the opportunity to identify the real effects of certain ways of being and of thinking on persons' lives and relationships is very important. To do this we need critical reflection, and for critical reflection we need history. History is doubly important, because it is largely through history that *unique outcomes* or *exceptions* render alternative stories. I emphasise largely, because developments that are projected into the future of a person's life also play a role in rendering unique outcomes into alternative stories. However, rarely is it difficult to achieve this storying of the unique outcome by a process of historicising. Even the fact that persons will judge these unique outcomes to be positive developments suggests that they must fit, in some way, with some prior conception that the person has of a better life. So, once articulated, it makes a lot of sense to show an interest in the history of such conceptions, and the experiences of life that relate to this. Through this exploration, exceptions or unique outcomes become deeply rooted. And, on reflecting on these alternative histories, it becomes possible for persons to identify preferred values and commitments in life. Perhaps the attention to history is one distinction between solution-oriented therapy and the narrative orientation that I and others have been developing. But it is not the only distinction.

Shelly: I wonder, also, if it's a distinction, between your work and that of others in this area that you attend to the "audience" or those people who may be affected by the re-storying, rather than simply focusing on the family you're working with?

Michael: This is a vitally important part of this work. If the stories that we have about lives are negotiated and distributed within communities of persons, then it makes a great deal of sense to engage communities of persons in the renegotiation of identity. So, regardless as to whether I am meeting with an individual, a couple, or a family, I am thinking about possible audiences to the unfolding developments of therapy, and thinking about how this audience might be invited to play a part in the authentication of the preferred claims that are emerging in the process of the therapy. And I am active in the generation of these possibilities for authentication, even if I never have the opportunity to meet with the persons who are invited to play this role. However, on many occasions I do have this opportunity and, as therapy proceeds, there are more and more and more persons in my counselling room whose direct contribution is acknowledged. In my efforts to track down the history of these alternative stories, I often come across persons who haven't been seen for years by the persons who are consulting me. We then, through establishing important reconnections, have some very, very moving experiences together. I really appreciate the opportunity to interview these persons "from the past" in the presence of those persons who have consulted me: *Look, I was talking to Jane and I asked her whether there was anyone in her life who could tell me a story that would help me understand how she took this recent step, and your name came up. She said she hadn't seen you for 15 years, and I'm really glad that she managed to catch up with you, and that you were enthusiastic about the idea of meeting with us. I just wonder if I could ask you a few questions about Jane. From your memories, what stories could you tell me about her that would help me understand how she took this step?* and so on. We usually find the responses of these persons from the past to be entirely invigorating.

Donald: So you're sort of a therapeutic anthropologist.

Michael: I'm not sure of this, but I really like the description.

Donald: Let's talk about the process of re-storying. How do you go about the process of creating a new story, or re-storying?

Michael: Well, I think that there are two things going on here. Life is multi-storied, not single-storied. Apart from the dominant stories of our lives, there are always sub-stories, and these sub-stories are relatively available to us in this work with individuals, couples, and families. Second, persons have many experiences of life that are not readily intelligible through the dominant stories or the sub-stories of their lives. It's the sub-stories themselves, and also these aspects of experience that stand outside of dominant stories and the sub-stories, that really provide a point of entry for re-authoring work. This is really what I'm focusing on.

Donald: My sense is that it involves a joint authorship between you and the family, with greater emphasis on the family's input - rather than you as therapist suggesting that *this* would be a good story.

Michael: Yes. I can ask lots of questions that have the effect of privileging these sub-stories and these neglected aspects of experience, but I can't fill in the details of the alternative landscapes of life that are associated with these. For example, I can be very curious about certain developments, about how certain events might be linked to other events, but I can't actually know how they might be linked, or what it is exactly that might link them, or the specific part that these events could play in an alternative conception of the progression of another person's life. I can ask questions about an event here, at this point in time, and about another event that occurred two months earlier that might be related to it in some way. Maybe: *What was it that prepared you for this step?* and *Could there be some connection between this and this other development of two months ago?* So, I can be curious about the links. I can be curious about other events that might, in some way, relate to what persons determine to be the preferred developments of their life - but I can't know the details. One outcome of this process is that persons begin to situate these other events of their lives in particular sequences of events across time.

At a point I usually encourage persons to reflect on these unfolding developments with the purpose of naming them. Perhaps I could say that this is like the naming of a "counterplot" or an "alternative plot" and, once done, this makes it possible for family members to actually give meaning to a variety of other experiences that fit with this alternative plot. It has been argued that memory is structured according to narrative, and in this work we so often see a restructuring of memory.

Donald: Do you think it's important that people name both of the plots - the dominant plot and the counterplot?

Michael: When persons present for therapy, discussion of the problem is informed by a narrative frame - by an account of events unfolding in a specific sequence across time and according to what I regard to be a dominant plot. In this work that I have been discussing here, there is at times a renaming of the dominant plot, but always a naming of a counterplot or alternative plot. This process of renaming and naming is really important. The naming of an alternative plot greatly facilitates the ascription of meaning to a whole range of experiences that have previously been neglected.

Donald: Your mode of working seems to consist, almost entirely, of questions. I was wondering, when you were talking about families being able to link this alternative story together, if you suggest those links through your questions?

Michael: Some sort of a link is suggested through the questions. Also, I'm playing an active part here in other ways as well. There may have been some pieces of information that persons have shared which I think might provide clues about the nature of the link, and I might say: *Well, does this fit? Could these two events be connected in some way?*

Donald: But, it would be unusual for you to say "This seems to fill the gap".

Michael: Well, at times I do, I hear myself saying something like this, and I don't always regret it.

Donald: That conforms to the idea that people validate their own lives. In terms of practice, does it reduce the likelihood that people will reject the idea if it is introduced as a question?

Michael: No, it is not a matter of whether or not persons will reject an idea, but a matter of relational politics. In fact, it is quite easy to impose ideas. It is very easy for us to impose "truths", because there is a power differential in our relations with those persons who seek help. If we can appreciate this, then it makes it more possible for us to take the steps to avoid the imposition of such "truths". This consideration informs more of a questioning approach to our work with persons. This consideration doesn't mean that I can't offer observations, but it does shape how I might offer these: *Well, I wonder if this experience could have played some part in this recent development, or do you think that it's entirely irrelevant to this? I've got these three ideas about the foundations of this recent step, but I'm not sure if any of them are relevant. I'm not sure if any of them provide reasonable clues to this recent achievement. Let me share the ideas with you, and then I can ask questions about what you think.* I think that the questioning approach relates to a commitment to a collaborative way of working with persons.

Shelly: I get the sense that you choose your words very carefully. Does this attention to word choice come also from the wish to avoid the abuse of power?

Michael: We have to be very sensitive to the issue of language. Words are so important. In so many ways, words are the world. So, I hope that a sensitivity to language shows up in my work with persons and, as well, in my writing. However, having said this, I'd probably now rewrite many things that I've written. I'd write them differently. [laughter] And, on reflection, I'd probably do this interview differently if we did it again.

Donald: We've spoken a little bit about re-storying or re-authoring here. One of the things that you've also talked about in this context are *landscapes of action* and *landscapes of consciousness*. Would you discuss those two concepts in relation to the re-authoring process?

Michael: I really borrow these terms from Jerome Bruner (1986) who, in turn, more or less borrowed them from a couple of literary theorists. The proposal is that stories have dual landscapes - landscapes of action and landscapes of consciousness, or, if you like, landscapes of meaning. The *landscape of action* is constituted by experiences of events that are linked together in sequences through time and according to specific plots. This provides us with the rudimentary structure of stories. If we drop one of those dimensions out - experiences of events, sequences, time, or plot - then we wouldn't have a story. These elements, together, make up the landscape of action. When persons come into therapy and talk about what they've come to see you about, they usually give an account of the landscape of action of the dominant story.

At this time, persons will also provide an account of the *landscape of consciousness* or the landscape of meaning of that dominant story. As they talk about certain events they will indicate what they think those events reflect about the character, motives, desires, and so on, of various persons in their social networks. They will also reflect upon what these events say about the qualities of particular relationships. So, the landscape of consciousness or meaning has to do with the interpretations that are made through reflection on those events that are unfolding through landscapes of action. To reiterate, the landscape of meaning is derived through reflection on events in the landscape of action to determine what those events might say about the desires, preferences, qualities, characteristics, motives, purposes, wants, goals, values, beliefs, commitments, of various persons. But here my account of this process is somewhat one-sided and simplistic. It obscures what is a recursive process, for the established accounts of characteristics, motives, commitments, and so on, inform the arrangement of experiences of events in the landscape of action.

In re-authoring work, we invite persons to traffic in both of these landscapes - by reflecting on what alternative events in the landscape of action might mean, and by determining which events in the landscape of action most reflect the preferred accounts of characteristics, of motive, of belief, and so on - so that alternative landscapes of action and of consciousness are brought forth. I know that it is often assumed that a motive is some sort of inner and relatively fixed force that determines a person's actions. But I believe that this view is untenable, that motives are not intrinsic and that they are not written in stone. Furthermore, I would argue that, because our lives are multi-storied, then we are all multi-motived, and that some of our motives have positive real effects in terms of our lives and in terms of our relationship ecologies, and some very clearly have very negative real effects.

Shelly: So, it seems that you need to progress in both of these areas simultaneously. If the landscape of action changes, but the way it is interpreted doesn't change, then it isn't really different.

Michael: Yes. I've been trying to emphasise what might be referred to as a "zig-zagging" process. We might be somewhere in history talking about what particular events might reflect: *Well, on reviewing these events that took place back then, what do they tell you about what you really believed was important in your life?* So, in referencing one landscape to another, we have jumped from landscape of action to landscape of consciousness. And we can go the other way: *Are you aware of any other developments in your life that reflect this particular belief about what is important to you?* So we are now back in the landscape of action.

This process can include a consideration of developments stretching into the near future of landscapes of action and of consciousness: *Just think about your next steps. Imagine that what we now understand to be important to you is going to feature more strongly in your life. How would this affect your actions regarding the issue that you have been concerned about? If you witnessed yourself taking these steps, how would this affect the picture that you have of yourself as a person? If you were to step more into this picture of who you are, what effect do you think this would have on your next steps?* or, *Assume that this clarity on what you have wanted for your life was to be influential with regard to future developments. What difference would this make to what happens in your life over the next week or two? If you were to acknowledge your own contributions to these developments, what would this tell you about what you are committed to? In knowing this, what difference do you think that this would make to how you might direct your life?* So here we have examples of referencing future developments in landscapes of action to alternative and historically-situated descriptions in landscapes of consciousness. Then, examples of referencing future developments in the landscape of consciousness to the descriptions of events in the alternative landscapes of action in the near future. And then examples of referencing future developments in landscapes of action to those descriptions in alternative landscapes of consciousness of the near future, and so on.

So I hope that this gives one account of what I am referring to when I'm talking about a "zig-zagging" process. However, in providing this example, I wouldn't want readers to assume that I follow any formal sequence of questions in this work, or to assume that there is a correct sequence.

Donald: Do you also move back and forth between past and future questions?

Michael: Yes. The movement isn't necessarily from recent or distant history to near future. In fact, on occasions this might be reversed.

Donald: You've mentioned that one of the ways that you keep change moving is to involve a larger circle of people in the change process. What are other aspects of how you keep the new narrative moving along?

Michael: Once established, these narratives go on providing an alternative frame for the attribution of meaning to those experiences of life that would otherwise have been neglected. And this continues to have real effects on life as lived. I know that this is putting it crudely, and that I generally eschew metaphors from the physical world, but a certain point is reached at which these stories appear to have a momentum of their own. As you have remarked, it is certainly important to be encouraging persons to identify and recruit some audience to the preferred developments of their lives - this is powerfully authenticating of these developments.

In this work, I'm interested in the metaphors of "solidarity", "alliance", "collaboration", and "affiliation". So there is a considerable focus on the identification of those persons who might contribute to preferred developments in the lives of others, and on how we might engage those persons in this project. Letters and other forms of documentation often help in the accomplishment of these goals.

Donald: I think our readers might appreciate an example of such documents.

Michael: Okay. I was consulted by a person who has a history of experiencing himself to be a spectacular failure as a person. This person, whom I'll call Harry, had a well-established and acknowledged psychiatric career, which included a number of hospital admissions following a series of what is commonly referred to as acute episodes. Harry had also collected several diagnoses through this career, from schizophrenia to manic depressive illness. Now, in our work together, he just stopped torturing himself. In his attempts to achieve a sense of moral worth in his community, he had been operating on his thoughts, his body, his lifestyle, his soul, and so on. He had been doing all of this in the name of self-possession, self-containment, self-dependence, and so on - nothing special, you know, just the sort of specifications for personhood that are valorised in our culture. Well, he quit. He suddenly resigned from all this, and instead began to respect and honour his protest to all of these requirements. As an outcome of this, all of those ambitions and expectations that were stretching him and stressing him, and contributing to a vulnerability to "acute episodes", were suddenly thrown overboard, without any apology, without any excuses.

It was a glorious moment, and together we laughed so much that we cried. I felt so privileged to be part of this. As an outcome of this, for the first time in Harry's memory, he experienced his life going forward in positive ways, and found the state of mind that he had been searching for over such a long time: "calm sensibleness". After a time, Harry was ready to take certain steps to introduce others in his community to his achievement, and to enlist them in his project. He believed that this would discourage others from subjecting him to inappropriate expectations, further reduce the stresses in his life, and contribute further to his quality of life. I suggested that he might best achieve this by a statement that gave details of his project and that extended to others an invitation to join him in this. So, after asking Harry a series of questions, we put together the following document:

Expectations and My Life:

1. *I've learned a lot about expectations and what they demand of people.*

2. *Expectations can have a very destructive effect on my life and on the lives of other people.*

3. *Expectations have me feeling bad about myself and pressing myself in unhelpful ways.*

4. *If you want to help me in my life then please don't pressure me and don't expect me to be someone else who you want me to be. This includes expectations about health - I won't be guilt's person.*

5. *If you would like, I will provide you with a further and fuller understanding about the effect of expecations on my life, about what expectations have done to my life in the past.*

6. *Thank you for your time.*

Harry went away with 30 signed copies of this document, and was successful in his efforts to engage others in the renegotiation of his identity, and in extending his chosen lifestyle of "calm sensibleness".

Donald: Apart from documents like these, you've also mentioned using letters in your work. In these letters, do you focus more on re-storying or on deconstruction, and how do you make those choices?

Michael: These decisions are really determined by where we are in the work itself, and by the feedback we receive from persons about what would interest them most. But I will make some general comments about these letters. These letters are not strategic letters, but are more-or-less an account of the developments that are unfolding in the therapy. So only very rarely do they include new information. The letters incorporate a heavy emphasis on a verbatim account of these developments.

One paragraph might start: *When we looked at the effect of this problem on your life, this is what you said ...* The next might begin: *There were some other developments that caught our attention in the meeting, and I asked you some questions about this. You came up with some advice to yourself, and this is what you said ...* In different letters there are different emphases. For example, in some letters considerable space might be allocated to the renaming the dominant plot. This would often be the case for those persons who have been recipients of abuse. So often, at the outset of therapy, these persons present a very negative account of themselves, and a version of the dominant plot that suggests a complicity in the very abuse that they have been subject to. The renaming of the dominant plot as one about survival in the face of torture, tyranny, exploitation, and so on, goes a long way to deconstructing those negative "truths" that these persons were recruited into as an outcome of the abuse. And for the dominant plot to be renamed in writing is entirely significant, and contributes to a form of testimony that can have the effect of substantially freeing persons from many of the real effects of the abuse that was perpetrated on their lives.

Donald: Could you talk a little bit about what you mean by the phrase "working behind the clients"?

Michael: In so many ways, it's very easy for us to get ahead of the persons who seek our help. And persons can't see ahead with any clarity if we are standing in the way blocking their view. So, it is more appropriate to be standing behind these persons, or even perhaps alongside them - not specifying how things should be in their lives, not prescribing a direction for their lives. Instead of getting ahead of persons, we can, in so many ways, ask persons to bring us abreast of developments in their lives, to catch us up with these. If we can consistently ask persons how it was that they took the step that they took, what foundations these steps depended upon, what were the real effects of these steps on their lives and relationships, and so on, then I believe that we are drawing distinctions that are experienced by persons as empowering rather than disempowering.

In "catching therapists up" on significant developments, persons achieve a good sense of how conditions might have otherwise been in their lives, and this distinction provides the basis for further actions of a preferred nature. On the other hand, if we get overly enthusiastic about developments, or embrace "pointing out positives" as a central metaphor in this work, we run the risk of contributing to distinctions that could be experienced as quite disempowering. Under these circumstances, it is so easy for persons to assume that the therapist believes that they have arrived at a point that these persons don't perceive themselves to be at, or for persons to assume that the therapist expects that they will soon take some steps that these persons don't really believe they are capable of. This sets the context for persons to experience failure, and for a dependence on the authority of the therapist in order to "get things right" in their lives. And the outcome of this is sure to be a deterioration in the state of affairs.

Donald: What are the limitations of the narrative approach?

Michael: Well, as I wouldn't define it as an approach, it's hard for me to talk about limitations in the usual way. Is this work better defined as a world-view? Perhaps, but even this is not enough. Perhaps it's an epistemology, a philosophy, a personal commitment, a politics, an ethics, a practice, a life, and so on. And, because whatever it is happens to be on intimate terms with recent developments in social theory that are generally referred to as "non-foundationalist" or perhaps "postmodern", then whatever it is also happens to be a theory.

So, perhaps I can best answer your question in this way. In this work, I do come up against my own personal limitations, which I then want to explore. These are limitations with regard to language, limitations in my awareness of relational politics, limitations in my capacity to negotiate some of the personal dilemmas that we are confronted with at every turn in this work, limitations of experience, limitations in my perception of options for the expression of certain values that open space for new possibilities, and so on.

I want to explore these limitations, by talking about them with those persons who seek my help, and by talking about them with other therapists, and through personal reflection, through reading, and so on. In exploring these limitations in this way, I can extend what for me were the previously-known limits of this work.

Donald: Would you speak a little about training? How do people go about learning more about this world-view, and how to use it productively?

Michael: Well, they might approach someone who's actually involved in stepping into and exploring this story about therapy and about life.

Donald: I'm sure they could go to Australia, to Dulwich Centre.

Michael: They could. But there are also many fantastic developments in this sort of work here in North America that readers could catch up on. There are many family therapists who are embracing the narrative metaphor and other recent developments in social theory and, as well, the notion that therapy is inevitably a political activity. And there are many institutes and agencies that are bringing exploration of the narrative metaphor together with social justice issues.

Donald: What would you suggest that people read?

Michael: To fill in some of the gaps that will be left for them after reading the transcript of this interview, could I suggest that they start by reading a chapter called *Deconstruction and therapy*? This appears in a book called *Therapeutic Conversations*, edited by Steven Gilligan and Reece Price, and published by W.W. Norton. Also included in this book is a commentary on this work by Karl Tomm, other chapters by therapists who are working with narrative and solution-focussed orientations, and some comparison of these two orientations. I would recommend this book highly. The same chapter, *Deconstruction and therapy* also appears in a book that I co-authored with David Epston. The title of this book is *Experience, Contradiction, Narrative and Imagination*, which is available from Dulwich Centre Publications in Vancouver, Canada[1]. This book includes a variety of chapters that focus on recent developments in this work, and I would also highly recommend this to those readers who are interested in filling some of the gaps left for them after reading the transcript of this interview. A good source for ongoing developments in this work is the *Dulwich Centre Newsletter*, which is in fact a quarterly journal, and is also available from the Vancouver distributor. And, of course, there is *Narrative Means to Therapeutic Ends*, which I co-authored with David Epston, published by W.W. Norton in 1990.

Donald: And then, were there questions you'd like to be asked? Is there something that we didn't ask about, that you would like to discuss?

Michael: No, I think you've really asked a whole lot of interesting questions. And I hope that my answers were interesting, and that I didn't belabour the point.

Donald: No, I don't think you did. And we and our readers are most grateful for the time you've spent with us. It's really important work that you're doing, and we have appreciated this opportunity to learn more about it. Thank you.

---

1. Dulwich Centre Publications, PO Box 34185 Station D, Vancouver, B.C. V6J 4N1, Canada.

REFERENCES

Bruner, J. 1986:
  Actual Minds: Possible Worlds. Cambridge, MA: Harvard
  University Press.
Chomsky, N. & Herman, E.S. 1988:
  Manufacturing Consent: The political economy of the mass media.
  New York: Pantheon Books.
Derrida, J. 1977:
  Of Frammatology. (G.C.Spivak, Trans.) Baltimore, MD: Johns
  Hopkins University Press.
Epston, D. & White, M. 1992:
  Experience, Contradiction, Narrative & Imagination. Adelaide:
  Dulwich Centre Publications.
Foucault, M. 1970:
  The Order of Things: An archaeology of the human sciences. New
  York, Randam House.
Foucault, M. 1973:
  The Birth of the Clinic: An archaeology of medical perception.
  London: Tavistock.
Foucault, M. 1979:
  Discipline and Punish: The birth of the prison. Middlesex:
  Peregrine Books.
Foucault, M. 1980:
  Power/Knowledge: Selected interviews and other writings. New
  York: Pantheon Books.
Foucault, M. 1984:
  The History of Sexuality. Great Britain: Peregrine Books.
Gilligan, S. & Price, R. (Eds) 1993:
  Therapeutic Conversations. New York: W.W.Norton.
White, M. & Epston, D. 1990:
  Narrative Means to Therapeutic Ends. New York: W.W.Norton.

2.   The Politics of Therapy*
*Interviewer: Lesley Allen***

Lesley: Okay then. For the readers, could you give a brief sketch of your latest work looking at the differences between *externalizing the problem* and *externalizing the internalized discourse*?

Michael: I'm not sure that there is a distinction to be made here. But I do think that the idea of externalizing internalized discourses provides for a more adequate description of what this work is all about. I think the main point about the externalizing conversation is that it introduces a different way of speaking about, and a different way of thinking about, that which is problematic - and, of course, a different way of acting in relation to that which is problematic. These are ways of speaking, thinking and acting that are at odds with the ways of speaking, thinking and acting that are associated with the internalizing discourses. In promoting these externalizing conversations, we are engaged in an activity that is not entirely a pro-cultural activity. To an extent, this activity challenges the taken-for-

---

*   Previously published 1993, in "Human Systems: The Journal of Systemic Consultation & Management", 4:19-32, and in 1994 in "Context: A news magazine of family therapy". (This interview was conducted in London, November 1992.)

**   Lesley Allen is a family therapist, trainer and freelance consultant in London. Previously she lived and worked in Adelaide, and there graduated from the Dulwich Centre Family Therapy Training Course.

granted reproduction of some cultural ways of speaking about our lives andour relationships. These externalizing conversations have the effect of deconstructing some of the "truths" that persons have about their lives and about their relationships - those truths that persons feel most captured by.

Lesley: Can you be a bit more particular about these cultural ways of speaking, thinking and acting - those that are associated with the internalizing discourses?

Michael: In the history of the world's cultures, I believe that these modern internalizing discourses have provided for quite a novel way of thinking about and speaking about oneself and others - a way of thinking and speaking that is period and culture specific, one that has developed over the last three hundred years in Western culture, one that is central in the construction of the modern subject.

Lesley: So, what are the implications of these internalizing discourses in terms of how people live their lives?

Michael: They are entirely significant, as they mostly constitute life as we know it. Perhaps I should also say that these internalizing discourses constitute our blindness to life as it is produced, and as we produce it. They have the effect of isolating persons from each other, and from the very contexts of their own lives. These discourses have provided for a way of speaking and thinking about life that erases context, that splits experience from the politics of local relationship. The nature of these politics is largely obscured, as are, by the way, the very practices of self and of relationship that are associated with these ways of speaking and thinking.

Lesley: Such as?

Michael: Well, I think Michel Foucault provides a very interesting account of the development of these ways of speaking and of these practices. I hesitate to say much about this here, because I don't think that I can do his thought much justice in the space of this interview, and also because there are learned persons in this field who are quite scandalised by my references to Foucault.

Lesley: Well, just say a little. I promise not to be too scandalised.

Michael: Okay, but don't try too hard. I've taken some solace in this scandalisation, perhaps because it discourages others from assuming that I am a "Foucauldian" - whatever that means. I would never identify myself in this way, and certainly wouldn't aspire to this.

Lesley: Alright, I won't try too hard.

Michael: Okay, but I am doing this on the basis of an understanding that I am doing it hastily and poorly - and possibly this might not come out as a very Foucauldian account of some of Foucault's thought.

Lesley: Okay, it's understood.

Michael: I think that some of the key words are *exclusion, objectification, subjectification*, and *totalisation*. The ways of thinking about and speaking about oneself and others, and the practices of relating to oneself and others - those that are associated with internalizing discourses - are all very much about the objectification or the "thingification" of persons. Over the past few hundred years, in our culture, this has been achieved, in part, by the exclusion of persons and groups of persons by ascribing to them a spoiled identity. Of course, there have been many great exclusions in the history of the world's cultures, but this modern exclusion was a different sort of exclusion - not an exclusion based on the absence of identity, not an exclusion based on absence of membership, but a grand exclusion based on the assignment of identity. A marginalisation of persons through identity.

Lesley: People considered insane, homosexuals, and so on?

Michael: Yes. Take, for example, the division of the sexualities. At a certain point in history, for the first time, a person's sexual preference was considered to speak of the truth of their identity, the core of their being. This ascription of identity through preference provided the basis for a totalisation of persons, and for a great exclusion - an extraordinary marginalisation.

Lesley: Say more about objectification.

Michael: The processes of the objectification of persons were aided and abetted by the developments in the technology of the government of persons, and through the rise of the scientific classification of the body, and of life itself. This made possible the location of what we call "problems" at specific sites of the body. So, at a certain point in history, the body became a very particular sort of thing, that it was not, and could not be, at an earlier point in history.

Lesley: So, this provides us with an account of the history of psychopathology, of the disorders and dysfunctions?

Michael: Yes, to an extent it helps us to understand the processes by which these were fabricated, and encourages us to trace the history of the real effects, the constitutive effects, of these fabrications on life as it is lived. To an extent, this also helps us to understand the development of the structuralist tradition of thought, without which the psychopathologies and disorders could not have been invented, and without which even "family dynamics" would be unthinkable. But Foucault says much more than this. He provides an account of how certain processes of power engage persons in the subjugation of their own lives - in specific actions or practices that relate to the government or the policing of their own lives.

Lesley: What's an example of this?

Michael: I think that we are all doing this. But there are extremes. I have, for a long time, considered anorexia nervosa as the pinnacle of achievement of this system of self-government, this system of modern power. Just consider the practices of self-subjugation that persons with anorexia nervosa are recruited into: the rigorous and meticulous self-surveillance, the various self-punishments of the body for its transgressions, the perpetual self-evaluations and comparisons, the various self-denials, the personal exile, the precise self-documentation, and so on. It is significant that it has mostly been women who have suffered from anorexia nervosa, and I think that this says a lot about how this modern system of power has been taken up in the domain of gender politics.

Lesley: Here, and in some of your writing, you appear to have an interest in the history of these sorts of ideas and these practices. How important is this to your work?

Michael: Yes, I do have this interest, and I think that it is very important. Without doubt, the psychologies and psychotherapies play an entirely significant role in the reproduction of the dominant culture. And, to a very considerable extent, this is entirely understandable. It is impossible for us to arrive at a vantage point from outside of culture - and therefore outside of language and known ways of life - by which we might review our culture. However, this fact does not condemn us to blindly reproducing culture, without any hope of refusing or protesting those aspects which we experience as problematic. It does not restrict us to the role of accomplice to this modern system of power - we can assist persons to challenge certain practices of power, and to refuse the sort of practices of self that we have just been talking about. We do not have to be entirely complicit with dominant culture - in fact, I think that we should make it our business to ensure that we are not so.

Lesley: So, what are our options?

Michael: Well, to understand that we cannot be neutral in our interactions with those persons who seek our help - to understand, to grasp the political nature, and the reproductive nature, of local interaction is of paramount importance. If we believe that it is possible for us to be neutral in this work, then our interactions with those persons who seek our help will tend to be more exactly, more perfectly, pro-cultural.

Lesley: What else?

Michael: I do think that we can render transparent many of the taken-for-granted practices of the culture of psychotherapy that are reproductive of problematic aspects of the dominant culture. In part, we can achieve this through critical accounts of the history of these ideas and practices, and by a review of the real effects of these ideas and practices on persons' lives. We can deconstruct these ideas and practices by stepping into alternative sites of cultures - we can take up vantage points, perhaps at the margins of culture, from which we might review these dominant and taken-for-granted ideas and practices. We can explore the alternative modes of life and of thought that are associated with these alternative sites of culture. We can solicit critical feedback from persons of other races, cultures and classes. We can openly acknowledge the political dilemmas that we face in our day-to-day work. And we can stretch culture by stretching language - we can extend the limits of the known through the imaginative use of metaphor, through the renewal of metaphor. I think that it was Richard Rorty who said that a "fact" is a dead metaphor. When a metaphor has been taken into regular use to the extent that it is taken literally, it dies and becomes a fact. Dead metaphors have no potential for generativity, for challenging the boundaries of the known.

Lesley: How do these considerations translate into your work? How might these ideas make a different to practices in the field of therapy?

Michael: Let's take a relatively straightforward example. Some appreciation of the history of the modern instrument of power that we call the "file" or the "casenote" - the central role it has played in the facilitation of social control and subjugation - would make it very difficult for therapists in this field to continue to engage in what Rom Harre called "file-speak". This consideration would discourage us from engaging in the sort of practices that make it possible for the file to have an independent life.

Lesley: Yes, but what if it is necessary to take notes, or if we deem it helpful to do so?

Michael: In the taking of notes that might be helpful or necessary - and, of course, we can challenge the necessary - we might restrict ourselves to the visible recording of what the therapist considers to be particularly significant verbatim comments - a recording that is undertaken in the therapy session itself. We would also encourage those persons who seek our help to take notes on what they believe to be significant. These notes can then be put together, perspectives compared, and the parties to the interaction can decide on their eventual fate. If for some reason it is desirable to make notes outside of the face-to-face meeting, for example reports and letters, then these can be forwarded to all parties to the interaction, so that they might make commentary - so that any documents record their responses, and suggested corrections, etc.

Lesley: And I suppose there are many other implications of these ideas in regard to the context of therapy.

Michael: We can make it our business to structure the context of therapy so that it is less likely to reproduce dominant cultural forms of organisation, including those that perpetuate hierarchies of knowledge, and other oppressive practices. And I think that whatever a "good" therapy is, it will concern itself with establishing structures that will expose the real and potential abuses of power in the practices of the good therapy itself.

Lesley: I can think of other considerations. Before, we were talking about anorexia nervosa, and I can understand how helping young women to identify and challenge the various practices of self-subjugation would be freeing of them.

Michael: Yes. Not freeing them to be truly who they really are, but, in fact, freeing them from the "real". And I would hope that the sort of considerations that we are discussing here might assist us to resist the great incitement of popular psychology to tyrannise ourselves into a state of "authenticity" - that these sort of considerations might open up certain possibilities for us to refuse "wholeness", to protest "personal growth", to usurp the various states of "realness". To open the possibilities for us to default, and to break from the sort of gymnastics that regulate these states of being, that make all of this possible.

Lesley: We've travelled a long way from where we started - that is, discussing externalizing conversations. Do I take it that you implied that these conversations were more effective in bringing forth the context of people's experience, including relational politics?

Michael: Yes, I believe so. Consider those persons who have survived abuse, but who have been recruited into a very negative story about who they are, and who engage in various of the well-established practices of self-abuse. How often do you hear these persons say things like: "I'm hateful. I deserved the abuse, I had it coming to me. Besides, no-one can be abused unless they let it happen, unless they want it." These persons are engaging in conversations with self and with others that internalize the locus of abuse and, with this, there can be no appreciation of context. Through this process, the fact that they are abused reflects on their identity - is a testimony to their desires and motives, to their purposes in life. Now, the introduction of externalizing conversations can disrupt this, can re-politicise what has been de-politicised. These persons can be interviewed about the effects of the abuse on their lives, about what it has talked them into about who they are, and so on. In turn, the real effects of these private stories can be explored. One of the outcomes of these conversations is a renaming of the dominant plot - away from personal culpability and towards "domination", "exploitation", "servitude", "erasure" and "torture". In exploring the processes by which persons were recruited into these very negative private stories of their lives, and the associated practices of self-abuse, they find themselves describing various of the tactics of power - tactics that historically isolated them from others, tactics that exiled them from their own bodies, and so on. What I am saying is that in re-situating the history of self-abuse in local relationship politics, it becomes possible for self-abuse to be read through a different frame of intelligibility, one that presents alternative interpretations of these acts. This frees persons to object and to dissent. And, as well, it opens up possibilities for persons to arrive at new alliances with the self, and at new distinctions around abuse and care - to discern, perhaps for the very first time, exploitation from nurture.

Lesley: Okay, but how do these conversations apply to specific phenomena? Take paranoia, for example. How do you bring forth the context of this?

Michael: If a person is totalised as "paranoid", I might ask them a series of questions like: "How did you get recruited into the sense that you are under surveillance?" In response to this question, persons speak of their experience more politically. Having said this, externalizing conversations are by no means the only route to deconstructing the truths that persons find so capturing of them, and by no means the only route to bringing forth the context of relational politics.

Lesley: So, you don't always engage persons in externalizing conversations?

Michael: No, certainly not. Many persons do not experience a totalisation of their identity through dominant truths and, as well, there are other ways of having political conversations. I've worked with Vietnam veterans who have been diagnosed with post-traumatic stress disorder - nicely pathologising of a great number of these men who cannot reconcile themselves with, who cannot countenance, what they witnessed and what they did in the theatre of war. For them, a diagnosis of "violated compassion" seems to provide a far more experience-near description of what they are suffering from, one that emphasises context, one that certainly implicates, but one that presents options for action of the nature of redress. And one that introduces these men to possibilities in the revision of their relationship with themselves. And I might also add that we have yet to fully acknowledge our community's complicity in sending these men to Vietnam, and we have yet to find an apology and a mode of apology that is appropriate for this.

Lesley: What you are saying really strikes a chord with my experience. When I'm externalizing the problem, and tracking or mapping out the effects of this on people's lives - what those real effects are - it seems to me that this brings into contention, even more so, various ideologies and classifications. How does that fit with you?

Michael: It fits really well. You know, I think it brings the world into therapy - and I think it makes the personal the political.

Lesley: Yeah. In my view, there has been a history of professionals engaging in therapeutic practices and ideas which have obscured from their view, or enabled them to avoid, socio-political factors and issues of power. I've heard it said that introducing such notions may 'burden' the person with more problems.

Michael: That's an extraordinary idea! [laughs]

Lesley: Have you heard this idea before?

Michael: Yes, believe it or not, I have. But we can see this idea contradicted at so many moments in our work with those persons who seek help. In fact, the opposite appears to be the case. It seems that a whole range of choices for action become available when the world is brought more explicitly into therapy. If we make the political decision to exclude the world from therapy, we can actually create extraordinary burdens for the families, couples and individuals with whom we work.

Lesley: In the workshop, you talked about the importance of sharing professional literature with people, to undermine the mystification of therapeutic knowledge, to make sure that knowledges are shared, and to challenge the therapist's privileged position in the therapeutic system. One of the examples that you gave was of a woman who had been diagnosed with depression and who was suicidal. In the work that you described, is this another example of bringing the world into therapy?

Michael: I guess it is. This woman had suffered a double injustice - first deceit, and then denied deceit. Seven years into her relationship, she had sensed a change in her partner, and had begun to feel a little out of sorts. In response to her questions he said that he had always recognised that she suffered from "insecurity", and suggested that it had to do with unresolved issues in her family of origin. The woman consulted a counsellor about this, but to no avail. As time wore on, she felt more ill at ease, and asked more questions: "Aren't you happy with me? Don't you love me any more?" The reply came back: "You really are getting worse, aren't you? If you keep mistrusting my motives in this way, you will ruin our relationship." The woman began to deeply mistrust her personal experience, and her sense of reality and, over time, became quite incapacitated. Eventually, I guess in responding to the perception of some sort of nuance, she summoned the strength to broach the question: "Are you having an affair?" "Oh, now you are getting paranoid as well", came the response. The woman was shattered and began to experience what is commonly referred to as agoraphobia. Then, at thirteen years into the relationship, the woman was presented with uncontestable evidence that her partner had been having a series of affairs over the six-year period. A crisis in the relationship ensued, and the couple went to counselling. The partner owned up to his infidelity, and promised that it would not happen again - he now wanted the couple to work on what he "hadn't been satisfied with about the relationship in the first place". The counselling went nowhere, and eventually the counsellor suggested individual therapy for the woman "to assist her to let go of the past". At this point, her partner left the relationship to more fully engage in the affair that he had apparently never intended to wind up. The woman mostly blamed herself: "If only I had forgiven him. If only I had been adequate", and so on. Three weeks after a failed attempt on her life, she was sitting in my office, presenting a highly negative account of her worth as a person. I said that there was something familiar about her story, and rustled up a copy of Gas and Nichols' article on "gaslighting", which is about this sort of double injustice - deceit and denied deceit - and its real effects. Reading this article, discussing it with me, and naming the particularities of her experience from this new perspective was transformative for this woman. Her depression resolved, and together we discussed the possibilities of redress. One outcome of this is that the woman sent a copy of Gas and Nichols' article to the previous counsellor, with a note attached: "for your education". She also sent him a further ten copies of this article, with another note: "for your waiting room". The effects of these and other acts of redress - not, by the way, acts of vengeance - were entirely invigorating.

Lesley: You also said that you give certain documents about the aims and intended effect of torture to the survivors of abuse - depersonalisation, and so on.

Michael: Yes. But I don't do this willy-nilly. No therapeutic practices should be re-traumatising of persons in any way. With preparation, and at the right time, these documents can be profoundly helpful to persons in bringing forth the politics of their experience and in the renaming of the dominant plot. And another part of what is important about this is the realisation that the survivors of torture also experience so much shame and hold themselves culpable for their own degradations.

Lesley: I'd like to ask you more about the politics of this work.

Michael: Okay, so long as you tell the readers of this interview that it would not be reasonable for them to develop totalisations, based on this discussion, of what I think about and what I do.

Lesley: You were saying today about working with a woman who had been given a diagnosis of schizophrenia, and you made the comment that you thought the 'voices' she was hearing were quite 'patriarchal'. Certainly, here in Britain, black people and ethnic minorities are overly represented in psychiatric institutions, prisons, etc. And I was thinking about their 'voices' and/or internalized discourse as possibly being quite 'racist' and therefore reinforcing of their experience of oppression.

Michael: Yes. And I think that we have a part to play, if invited to do so, in working with these people to help "unpack" these voices.

Lesley: Voices of self-hate?

Michael: Yes, mega self-hate. Self-hate that has these people committing acts of self-destruction, sometimes acts of violence against themselves and, very often, against their own communities. To unpack the voice and those acts, to work together to identify the multiplicity of incitements experienced by these persons to act against themselves, and to identify the relations of domination and the subjugating practices of self that these persons have been recruited into. Rage becomes outrage, and this can be honoured. And it can be taken up as persons work to challenge specific injustices, with the aim of achieving at least a degree of redress. Having said this, I know that there is some risk that I will be perceived to be making sweeping generalisations about the hospitalisations and imprisonments to which you refer. I know that there is also much more to it, to the background of all this - including those inequalities that relate to the actual material conditions of these people's lives, current abuses of power and privilege, a general ignorance of the imperatives of other cultures, policies of admissions and confinements that disadvantage minority groups, a resistance to the requirements of the dominant culture, and so on.

Lesley: In thinking about this, given that the dominant Western culture is white, and patriarchal, do you as a white man make your position explicit when working with others from different cultural and racial backgrounds? Is this addressed?

Michael: The onus is on me to acknowledge the significance of my own race and ethnic location in the social world. And the extent to which I cannot assume an understanding is explicitly addressed. I acknowledge the extent to which I live in a distinct social domain, and I communicate the fact that I don't necessarily expect that others will take on the burden of catching me up with their experience in life in another distinct social domain. However, if they are willing to do so, then I would find this very helpful. But I think that it is also of critical importance to refer to cultural consultants. Over the past two years I have been consulting to an Aboriginal health service over the development of a counselling project - one that is culturally appropriate to the urban Aboriginal culture. This project was initiated from the recommendations that came out of an inquiry into Aboriginal deaths in custody. Now, I don't imagine that I could institute even one idea in this project that would not require mediation through Aboriginal knowledges.

Some people here in Britain probably know about the work of Charles Waldegrave, Kiwi Tamasese, Wally Campbell, Flora Tuhaka, and others, of The Family Centre in Wellington, New Zealand. Their work is unique in that they have developed various structures in efforts to assure culture, race, and gender accountability.

Lesley: Yes, there is a lot of interest in their work here, and I think their ideas and practice of cultural and gender accountability are very important and innovative. Can you say a little about the work in the Aboriginal Counselling Project?

Michael: I don't wish to say much about the specific developments in this project. To say something significant about this would require me to talk at some length about what I have learned about Aboriginal knowledges, and I have not been authorised to do so. As well, so many white people have been given privileged access to information and to life in the Aboriginal community, and have gone on to make success out of this - acknowledgement, honour, degrees, careers, and so on - and have returned nothing. This is a further injustice. Even without participating in this, as a member of the white culture, I know that I have a lot to return, and this weighs on me heavily, as it should. Perhaps the best way that I could respond to your questions is to take it back to the Project, and you might get a response.

Lesley: You were talking today about team-work and how, due to time restraints and the pressure of commitment, teaching, etc., you don't currently work with an ongoing team. If you did, what effect do you think it would have on you and your work?

Michael: I think it would have a very positive effect. It's a considerable gap in my working life, and has been for a long time. I've worked with many teams in training and consultation capacities, and have enjoyed this greatly, but haven't been part of a regular team since, let me see, around 1978 - that's 14 or 15 years ago. I think team-work is very generative, so it's a gap I'd like to fill, and I'm bound to do so at some point in the future.

Lesley: If that were to happen, would you be thinking about issues of gender and cultural balance in the team?

Michael: I'd certainly be thinking about balance, in terms such as these, in the team. Whether that translates into exact numbers is another question. I guess there are different ways of translating that.

Lesley: When I introduced you, I described you as a "well-watered plant" changing shape over time. That's my description, not yours, but would it be an "experience-near" description for you?

Michael: The watered part is quite experience-near, since I like to keep fit through swimming, which I also find meditative. The idea of changing and exploring and extending the previously-known limits of this work also fits. I figure that, if I came back to Britain at another time and did another workshop much the same as this last one, I'd like you to just tap me on the shoulder, tell me that this was the case, and I'd politely say "thank you" and quit. [laughter] I'd stop doing workshops. Or, if I ever came back to Britain and presented video-tapes of my work of two years before, and told you that "I would do exactly the same now", then I would invite you to openly wonder about this - and this would hopefully give me the courage to retrieve my critical perspective, and to try to work out why I was still complicit with what I was complicit with two years ago - perhaps in terms of processes of power, the reproduction of negative aspects of dominant culture, and so on - and why I was limited by the same possibilities that I was limited by two years ago.

Lesley: I'll keep this in mind, but I expect that you will deprive me of the opportunity. You mentioned David Epston's work in the workshop. I know that he lives in Auckland, New Zealand - a very great distance from Adelaide. How did you first come across each other?

Michael: Well, although we had previously exchanged a couple of letters, our first face-to-face contact was in 1981 at the Australian Family Therapy Conference. In the press of the crowds bustling between workshops, I heard people saying there was this extraordinary and irregular guy who was doing these extraordinary and irregular things in his work. Although I was involved in the organising committee for the conference and had certain responsibilities, I just abandoned things and went along to the workshop. There was David, and extraordinary he was - and, I would add, still is. Afterwards we talked about ideas and practices, experienced a camaraderie, and went on to develop a close friendship. Later we adopted each other as brothers.

Lesley: We are running out of time, but I have a couple more questions to ask. Sometimes I have ideas and engage in practices that are at variance with the dominant ideas and practices that I witness being performed around me, in the contexts in which I work and circulate. And, despite positive feedback from families about my preferred ideas and practices, it's difficult sometimes to prevent these ideas and practices from being eroded by what could be described as certain processes of disqualification or subjugation. I imagine that you've come across these difficulties yourself, and I wonder how you manage it, so that your preferred ideas and practices do not suffer this erosion?

Michael: That's a hard question to answer here because there is such a big answer and, as you have said, we have such little time. So, perhaps I'll restrict my response to the sustenance that I get from the interaction with those persons who seek my help. Inevitably, we change each other's lives, often in ways that are hard to speak of. But I think that an awareness of the contributions that all of the parties to this interaction make to each other's lives is very important. And, here I would particularly like to emphasise the importance, to me, of acknowledging the ways in which these interactions are life-changing for me - the importance of finding an appropriate way of openly speaking of this within the therapeutic context. In saying this, I am precisely not talking of anything ingratiating, nor am I proposing any dramatic gesture. And I am definitely not proposing something that has some strategic aim, like a one-down position for therapists, which I believe to be ingenuine, patronising, and disqualifying. But, instead, perhaps to comment on a new perspective I might have gained on something, and what this might mean to my work with other families, or to my approach to my own life. Or perhaps about what I've learned to appreciate that I might have found difficult to appreciate at another time, and how this might have personally affected me. Or perhaps to comment on what I might have experienced as a "gift" - maybe a word or a phrase that provides me with a new "thinking tool", or maybe the privilege of witnessing certain developments that are generally evocative of other ways of being, or new possibilities, and so on. To identify this, and to articulate it in the therapeutic context is somehow very sustaining. But this is not all, and you have raised such an important issue at the end of the interview, that I am thinking we should start all over again and put this question first!

Lesley: Just one last question. In the workshop, you also reflected on your value position, particularly mentioning the notions of "commitment" and "solidarity". I guess that some clear acknowledgement and an ongoing appraisal of one's preferred values also counters demoralisation?

Michael: Yes. Critical to this, in fact. But I was referring to values with a small "v" - not those that propose, or are based on, some universal notion of the good, and not those that establish some normalising judgement of persons. Rather, I think that I was referring to an ethical position. But that's another story - one, by the way, that Karl Tomm has had a good deal to say about in recent times.

Lesley: It's time for us to go. Thank you so much. I have found this discussion useful and inspiring, and look forward to hearing more this afternoon.

Michael: And I've enjoyed the opportunity to catch up with you again Lesley, this time in London.

REFERENCES

Gas, G.Z. & Nichols, W. 1988:
    "Gaslighting: A marital syndrome." **Contemporary Family Therapy,** 10(1).
Madigan, S.P. 1992:
    "The application of Michel Foucault's philosophy in the problem externalizing discourse of Michael White." **Journal of Family Therapy,** 14(3).
Waldegrave, C. 1990:
    "Just Therapy." **Dulwich Centre Newsletter,** 1:5-46. (A special issue on social justice and family therapy, a discussion of the work of The Family Centre, Lower Hutt, New Zealand.)
White, M. 1989:
    "The externalizing of the problem and the re-authoring of lives and relationships." **Dulwich Centre Newsletter,** Summer 1988/89.

White, M. 1992:
> "Deconstruction and therapy." In Epston, D. & White, M. (co-authors), **Experience, Contradiction, Narrative & Imagination.** Adelaide: Dulwich Centre Publications.

White, M. 1992:
> "Men's culture, the men's movement and the constitution of men's lives." **Dulwich Centre Newsletter,** Nos.3&4.

White, M. & Epston, D. 1990:
> **Narrative Means to Therapeutic Ends.** New York: W.W. Norton.

3.   Outside Expert Knowledge*
*Interviewer: Andrew Wood***

Andrew: When we had lunch together last week, I was interested to hear that your past had included working as a clerk, and that you also loved surfing. How did you find your way into family therapy?

Michael: In about 1967, I started working as a clerk in what was then the Department of Social Welfare. At that time, this was one of the few places that one could work and also study social work at the same time. Before that, I had a brief stint working as a draftsman for an electrical engineering company.

Andrew: That seems a far cry from where you ended up.

Michael: I wound up training as an electrical and mechanical draftsman because I went to a vocational counsellor when I was at school. It was the thing to do in those days. He told me that I needed to do something with my hands as well as with my head. His tests told him that I was suited to the engineering field, despite the fact that I had never been interested in

*   Previously published 1991 in the "Australian & New Zealand Journal of Family Therapy", 12(4):207-214.

**   Chief Social Worker, Child & Adolescent Mental Health Service, Flinders Medical Centre, Bedford Pk 5042, South Australia.

this. At the time, I didn't have any strong ideas about what I should do, so, before I knew it, I found myself working and studying in a field that I felt was entirely inappropriate for me. So I left.

Andrew: So, why social work?

Michael: I think that I started social work training in 1967, and there were many factors behind this decision, some of them fortuitous. In the space that we have for this interview, it would not be possible for me to detail all of these. I was certainly interested in working with people. This appealed to me far more than the idea of working with machines. And I can recall that the idea of counselling attracted me back then.

Andrew: The first time I came across your name was in my social work training, when we were shown a film you were associated with: *They Reckon a Woman's World's Just It and a Bit* (South Australian Film Corporation, 1976). Community development and social action were vague notions for me, until I saw that film.

Michael: That project grew out of some multiple family therapy groups that I had organised in 1973 and 1974 at Hillcrest Hospital. These groups were attended by families which had members who were, or had been, patients of the hospital. At the end of one of the series of these meetings, the women in the group decided to continue to meet to support each other, and asked me if I would be able to join their meetings. A decision was taken to hold these meetings in the community in which most of the women lived - a relatively poor and under-serviced housing trust community. The principal of the local primary school was enthusiastic about the idea, and made a room available for the meetings.

In the first place, the group put their energies into supporting others in the community who were struggling under great hardship, mostly sole women parents. From there, the group went on to social action as a means of addressing some of the needs of their community. They became quite militant. For example, they blocked the traffic on a busy highway next to a primary school in order to get some action going on a school crossing for children. Children had been knocked down here, but there had been no response from the local authorities. They got their crossing.

I was actively involved with this group for some period of time, responding to the requests of the members to assist in their planning, and in the articulation of their philosophy. These were spirited meetings, in which an atmosphere of generosity and camaraderie prevailed. We all learned a lot from each other about the many possibilities for a better existence, and about the extent to which people can act together to breathe life into these possibilities.

Andrew: Do you agree with the criticism, often emanating from social work, that family therapy has been too family-centred and disregarding of community and social action?

Michael: I think that it can be fairly said that family therapy has been family-centred to the point that its practitioners have, at times, been oblivious to the wider social and political realities that frame its existence. However, I do meet many family therapists who are actively addressing these wider issues in their work with families. I think that the development of the more critical "constructivist" perspectives, and the decline of the more "positivist" models is facilitating this shift. This comment may surprise some readers, as many therapists in our community appear to confuse constructivism with relativism, or nominalism, to which, however, it bears no relation.

Andrew: Your teaching trips overseas have become more frequent over the last few years. How have you experienced the transition from teaching in Australia and New Zealand to teaching overseas?

Michael: Initially it was a bit anxiety-provoking. But I've found that doing workshops overseas is not all that different. There are cultural differences in patterns of audience response, and it sometimes takes me a while to situate these responses within cultural contexts. For example, in some places it is a standard practice for workshop participants to eat and drink during workshops, and it took me a while to accommodate to a "sea of chomping faces". What did this say about my workshop? Nothing, it turned out, except that the participants felt comfortable. In some other places, participants remain in their seats and talk animatedly together instead of going for a tea break. So I find it helpful to ask local family therapists to interpret these phenomena for me.

Andrew: What is your sense of how your ideas and style of therapy are accepted overseas?

Michael: There does seem to be a strong interest in what I am saying in terms of ideas, particularly those that relate to the narrative metaphor, and those that relate to fields of power. In terms of "style of therapy", perhaps interest is turning towards those approaches that are considered to be more "collaborative" and less imposing. I might add that I do not think that these developments in my ideas and practices are at all isolated. I think other therapists have been interested in my work to the extent to which it fits with, and assists them to build upon, their own preferred values and practices, even if they have not articulated these very completely.

Andrew: Not including your teaching at Dulwich Centre, would you be doing more teaching overseas than in Australia and New Zealand?

Michael: Yes, I probably would be.

Andrew: That brings me on to how you situate yourself in family therapy in Australia. It seems you've taken a lower profile over the last few years.

Michael: Yes, I have actually.

Andrew: Has that been a conscious decision on your part?

Michael: Pretty much so. After the 1985 Melbourne conference, I decided that I would take a lower profile generally in family therapy in Australia if I could achieve this.

Andrew: Has this suited you?

Michael: Yes, it has been the right thing to do. There seemed to be some complex feelings on behalf of some family therapists about the extent to which I was perceived by others to hold a certain position in the family therapy field in Australia and New Zealand. I didn't want to participate in this. And, as well, it seemed to me that the attention my work was receiving meant that a lot of other people's work wasn't getting the wider recognition it deserved. I think that this has now changed a lot - there seems to be a much more general recognition of the unique contributions made by many family therapists in Australia and New Zealand.

Andrew: Has your decision to take a lower profile in Australian family therapy and its politics had a counter-side at all?

Michael: No, not at all. I think it has been positive all round. And I still experience a great deal of enthusiasm for what I am doing, and I very much appreciate this support. But the enthusiasm is spread around more generally now, which is how I think it should be.

Andrew: I'm interested in talking to you a little about how your theoretical position has changed, particularly over the last decade. It seems to me that roughly the first half of the 1980s was characterised by your proposal of a therapeutic metaphor largely informed by cybernetics and Bateson, with the last few years more influenced by the ideas from text and narrative theory.

Michael: It's probably not that clear-cut. I have experienced a number of shifts in my thinking, but these shifts mostly do not constitute definitive breaks. And some of the earlier cybernetic metaphors still seem helpful to families. For example, David Epston and I are currently putting the finishing touches to an article on children's feeding difficulties. This work is partly informed by the "feedback as restraint" metaphor, and has changed little over the past 10 years.

I was very interested in Bateson's notion of "restraints of redundancy", and in the exploration of how these restraints act to determine what persons select out, from the random, for survival - of the part that these restraints play in evolution in determining what events or experiences persons attend to and how they respond to these.

A consideration of Bateson's restraints of redundancy introduced me to interpretive structures and to meaning as the heartland of life as we know it. How far away from these considerations does the narrative metaphor take us, in proposing that our lives are constituted by the meanings we give to experience, as we interpret these experiences through the stories that we have about our lives? The answer is surely that it does take us somewhere different, but in my mind this is not a place that is sharply discontinuous, and it certainly hasn't been so, for me, in regard to practice.

Andrew: What has the narrative metaphor meant for your thinking and your work?

Michael: Some years ago Cheryl White and David Epston urged me to consider the narrative metaphor as an interpretive structure for the work that I was doing. In responding to this, I developed a second description of a whole range of therapeutic processes. For example, it enabled me to conceive of "relative influence" questioning from a different angle. Those questions that encourage family members to map the influence of the problem in their lives I interpreted as deconstructive - these questions serve to deconstruct the dominant and impoverishing stories that persons are living by. And those questions that invite family members to map their influence in the "life" of the problem I interpreted as reconstructing, or re-authoring.

This and other reinterpretations provided by a consideration of the narrative metaphor have enabled me to further explore and extend the limits of this work. In fact, it has enabled me to transgress what I previously experienced as these limits.

Andrew: I experience the narrative metaphor in therapy as being more human, more honest.

Michael: This metaphor requires that the therapist challenge his/her settled certainties. S/he can't know, in advance, what's "right" for people - can't even know how the family "should" look at the end of therapy. The narrative metaphor challenges totalising practices. It encourages the therapist to enter into a reflexive position in relation to the constitution of therapeutic realities. And it encourages the therapist to assist those persons who seek therapy to enter into a similar position in relation to their own lives and, as well, to engage in the re-authoring of their lives according to alternative and preferred stories about who they might be.

In my view, this re-authoring process is not like the technique of reframing, in which the onus is on the therapist to develop a new and better story about the person's experience. Instead, it is a process that engages all persons actively in "meaning-making", and one in which there is a concerted effort on behalf of the therapist to privilege family members as the primary authors of these alternative stories.

Andrew: Do you have some directions of inquiry that you want to pursue with the narrative metaphor?

Michael: I'm certainly thinking of pursuing the narrative metaphor further. There is much more exploration to be done. I'm also interested in working further with the contributions of critical theorists, like Michel Foucault, and, as well, in studying the work of a number of literary theorists.

I would like to think that I have a "critical constructivist" or "constitutionalist" perspective. When I think about the constitution of persons' lives, if I were to limit my perspective to the narrative metaphor, then I believe that I would be losing a lot of the picture. As I have mentioned in several publications, and following Foucault and others, I believe that constructs "survive" in fields of power. This consideration behoves me to undertake some analysis of events in terms of practices of power, social structures, and so on, and in terms of the history of these practices and of the development of these structures.

For example, in regard to practices of power, I do not believe that it is by chance that, in our modern culture, couples mostly get into highly adversarial interactions at separation over property, maintenance, custody and access. Each couple doesn't dream up the well-known moves and countermoves of these adversarial practices by themselves. And I do not believe that these practices can be reduced to constructs - they are about know-how.

While on the subject of ideas, I might say that I do not think that the study of ideas has led me to the invention of specific therapeutic practices. I believe that such practices are generated in the to-and-fro of the interaction between the therapist and the persons who seek therapy. And we are very much dependent on the feedback of these persons to know which practices are helpful and which are not. However, I believe that the study of ideas contributes rigour to our thinking, and helps us to further understand, to explore the limits of, and to extend these practices.

Andrew: Given that so many of the difficulties that family therapists work with are situated in these cultural practices, it strikes me that family therapists on the whole don't say much publicly about them.

Michael: No, I don't think we do. And there is much to be said about them. Take men who are abusive of women and children. They are not just suffering an attitude problem. They are participating in a particular way of being that includes the subjugation of others through various well-known and well-established technologies of power - such as surveillance, comparison, inconsistency, isolation, and so on. So, I am proposing that we take a closer look at the practices that accompany particular knowledges of "ways of being" in this world.

Andrew: In regard to your reference to power and its place in constructivist thought, I'm interested in your thoughts on Maturana's constructivism. Borrowing heavily from biology, he describes human systems as informationally closed and internally wired. In a recent article,

Lyn Hoffman (1990) expressed some discomfort with this "black box" image, arguing that it ignores the interactional element in the construction of meaning. What's your view on this?

Michael: I don't know very much about Maturana, so cannot comment on his potion. However, I have no doubt that people can and do influence each other. In fact, some people specialise in influencing others, and appear to do it extraordinarily well. History is replete with examples of people being influenced to do things that are "against their better judgement", against what they would do "under ordinary circumstances". It also seems patently obvious that there exist enormous structural inequalities in this world. And this means that there are some people who can do some things to other people who cannot do them back because of the inequalities perpetuated by these structures.

Andrew: Are family therapists doing enough to address these inequalities?

Michael: I think that some family therapists have made a good start, particularly in terms of addressing gender issues. There is also more attention being given to racial inequalities, poverty, and other social justice issues. I think that the culture of family therapy is changing in some ways, and I know that Charles Waldegrave and the group from The Family Centre, Lower Hutt, New Zealand, have had a lot to do with this. However, there is still so much for us to do in raising our consciousness about these issues.

Andrew: I'd like to get back to how the ideas of narrative and re-authoring are influencing the way you practice with families. In particular, could you talk more specifically about how you participate with families in therapy?

Michael: One practice that has become very important to me is inviting persons to interview me about the interview itself. I will ask if any of my comments or questions seemed unclear, or if any of these led to any uncertainty or confusion about my purposes, and so on. I then encourage persons to ask me questions about all of this so that I might render my participation more transparent. My response is not in terms of some theoretical "truths", but in terms of how I believe the expression of my personal experience, imagination, and intentional states, has shaped my questions, comments, etc.

Andrew: Are you doing this in every session?

Michael: Sometimes there are contingencies that prevent this, but I make this invitation nearly all of the time now. Of course, sometimes it is necessary for the therapist to assist persons to enter into the spirit of this: "I thought that you might have been curious to know where I was coming from when I asked this question". In this way the therapist's participation can be deconstructed - it becomes situated.

This practice also makes it less likely that people will experience being imposed upon in therapy. If I make a comment that comes across as a strong opinion about what a person or a family should do, and if there is no opportunity for me to deconstruct this, then it only leaves the person or the family with the choice of either submitting to my opinion or railing against it. If, however, I have the opportunity to situate this comment within the context of my personal experience, imagination, and intentional states, then persons can determine for themselves how they might take the comment. This opens many possibilities for dialogue and for the consideration of alternative views and opinions.

I've had some very good feedback about this practice, and some persons tell me that, for them, this was one of the most important parts of the interview. This sure challenges the idea, popular in some circles, that for therapy to work it is important that persons do not know what the therapist is up to.

I also routinely encourage persons to evaluate the interview to determine what parts of it were relevant to them, which parts were not so, and what they found helpful and what they didn't. As persons respond to this, those viable points of entry for re-authoring processes become abundantly clear. For example, I can enquire about why a particular comment was helpful, explore any realisations that might have accompanied this, and encourage persons to speculate about the possible real effects that might be associated with such a realisation - how this might contribute to the shape of their life, etc.

Andrew: This practice seems to be a way of taking some of the guesswork out of ascertaining the meaning of therapy for families.

Michael: Yes, it does. It enables people to tell the therapist about the real effects of the interview, the meaning that they ascribe to events, and encourages them to help the therapist to determine what might be the best focus.

Andrew: This interviewing of you by the family must make you more accountable.

Michael: I think accountability is a big part of this practice. If we are more in touch with the real effects of the way we talk with families, and of the questions we ask, then I think we can be more accountable. This confronts us with the moral and ethical responsibilities associated with our participation with persons who seek therapy.

Andrew: You also seem to be describing a therapy that is more egalitarian.

Michael: There is much that we can do to make the therapy context more egalitarian. However, I think it's an error to believe that therapy can ever be totally egalitarian, because the very structure of this context builds in what might be referred to as a power differential. To blur this distinction, and to enter the belief that therapy can be totally egalitarian, would make it possible for therapists to ignore the special moral and ethical responsibilities associated with their position. However, taking this into account, I do believe that we should do what we can to make it very difficult for that power differential to have a toxic or negative effect.

Andrew: How are you incorporating the use of teams into the thinking and practice you have been describing?

Michael: I've been experimenting with the reflecting team in a number of ways. At the point in the interview at which the family and the regular therapist become the audience, I encourage the team members to interview each other about their reflections. This way, the whole session becomes a series of interviews. If one team member comments on what they consider to be a significant event that might relate to those developments that family members have judged to be preferred, then rather than the other team members simply agreeing with her or him, they can ask that team member what it was exactly that caught their attention, why they thought the development to be significant, and what they intended in making these comments in the reflecting team context.

Apart from the various possibilities that this opens for the team members to contribute to the co-authorship of alternative and preferred stories, it provides the opportunity for team members to situate their interest within the context of their personal experience, imagination, and intentional states. This interviewing in the reflecting team context is highly authenticating of the team members' comments, curiosity, and so on.

Andrew: It reflects a shift away from team anonymity and anonymous comments.

Michael: Anonymity doesn't exist in the team practice I'm describing. Before team members begin their reflections, they introduce themselves to the family members and give a little information about the background of their interest in this work.

Andrew: This practice would render the team more accountable as well.

Michael: Yes. Team members become more aware of and more appreciative of the degree to which their position is a privileged one in relation to the extent to which persons open their lives to them. Also they are less likely to get "ahead" of the family members, and less likely to respond in ways that are disconnected from their experience. I was interested to read your article on one-way screens that appeared in the *Dulwich Centre Newsletter*, and wasn't at all surprised that families often respond negatively to the experience of the anonymous and autonomous team. In contrast to this, it is interesting that those families that have experienced the teamwork I have been describing are invariably more enthusiastic to book their next appointment with a team than without. And I believe that this has a lot to do with the team's accountability to the family.

Andrew: The reflecting team seems to be another practice in family therapy that directly challenges the idea that a therapist or group of therapists can objectively know another person's experience and what is good for them. The interesting contradiction for me is that this is occurring in a society where helping professionals are becoming increasingly proclaimed, and proclaiming themselves, as experts in other's lives. How do you deal with this contradiction?

Michael: To some extent, we are all trained in these expert views, and can easily fall into the trap of believing that we possess "truths" that should be privileged above other knowledges. When this happens, we lose sight of the fact that these "truth" claims are actually specifying of certain norms for how persons should live their lives. In the training context, it is important to find ways of helping participants to put these expert knowledges in brackets. I guess this also holds true for the self-knowledges of the participants. I'm not assuming that it is possible for us to live a life that is not mediated by constructed knowledges, but it is important that we don't wind up specifying the lives of others through these knowledges. So, part of the training context is structured to assist participants to render visible those modes of life and thought by which they live their lives.

Andrew: Some would wonder what we'd be left with if expert knowledges were tucked away in brackets.

Michael: I think it's important to draw a distinction here between the idea of skills on the one hand, and expert knowledges on the other. By skills, I mean particular practices that therapists can and do make it their business to develop, such as those that establish therapy as a context for the re-authoring of lives and of relationships. The dialogue that is informed by these skills is usually, but not always, distinct in relation to the dialogue one might have with a friend or neighbour.

Andrew: The distinction you're making is that we can pursue these skills and learn to use them effectively, but not perceive ourselves as knowing the truth about how people should be.

Michael: That's right. For example, take what I refer to as re-authoring practices. Therapists can identify certain contradictions to the problem-saturated stories that persons bring to therapy. However, it is not possible for the therapist to determine whether these contradictions represent preferred developments, or to unravel, in any detailed and particular way, the mysteries associated with these contradictions. This is only something that family members can do from their lived experience and their imagination as they respond to the therapist's curiosity. And, in so doing, they resurrect and/or generate alternative and preferred knowledges of ways of being.

By the way, I believe that this work can be defined as interactional in a number of ways, but not according to the orthodox definition of interactional approaches. In regard to premises about interaction, the proposal here is not that idiosyncratic interaction is at the "root" of the problem, but that interaction is prefigured on meaning-making, and also founded on cultural practices. And, in regard to the actual process of therapy, family members and therapist engage in a variety of interactions of a co-authoring nature.

Andrew: So interaction doesn't just originate out of the blue.

Michael: Yes, that's the idea.

Andrew: In some of your writings, you have suggested that the skills of a good writer and the skills of a good therapist are analogous. It seems to me that family therapy is rapidly moving away from the system metaphor and embracing ideas and values from literature, philosophy, and so on, where such qualities as intuitive knowledge are receiving greater recognition.

Michael: A shift in thinking is certainly occurring. This is a shift away from the previously dominant metaphors of therapy that recruit the therapist into the so-called expert role. As therapists begin to consider some of the more recent developments in social theory, I believe that the shift towards metaphors from the domains of literature, philosophy, anthropology, and so on, will become even more significant.

Andrew: In relation to the constitution of lives, you have on several occasions mentioned the place of imagination. What is the connection between the constitution of lives and imagination?

Michael: A year or so back, I was introduced to the work of Gaston Bachelard, and I found him very interesting on the subject of imagination. He starts out by discussing different versions of imagination, including the one that proposes that images somehow reflect what has gone before. This is the version of imagination that is dominant in the analytic view. Bachelard juxtaposes these other versions of imagination with one that he regards as constitutive. This constitutive imagination is activated by reverie, a phenomenon that he regards to be of a nature entirely distinct in relation to "night dreaming". The state of reverie can be triggered by a range of experiences, from reading poetry to walking in forests. And I am sure that it can also be triggered by some of the evocative languages of therapy.

Andrew: You're not talking about the imagining of what has gone before, but rather the imagining of what could be.

Michael: Yes. Bachelard is referring to images that might be transformative of lives. But he is not just proposing that these images are future-oriented. He refers to the images of reverie as reverberations, and argues that events or experiences of the past resonate with these. So he is talking about images that reach back instead of images that come forward and primarily represent something past.

Andrew: How does this connect with constructivist thought?

Michael: Well, I feel like saying don't quote me on this, because I am not as well acquainted with Bachelard's work as I would like to be, and I don't know that I have thought through the implications of these ideas all that thoroughly. But I was very attracted to these ideas, and there seemed something almost familiar about them. And when I say something almost familiar, I'm not referring to Bachelard's reference to Jung, to whom I do not at all feel connected.

I think that these ideas struck a chord for me in relation to what I call re-authoring practices. In this work, the therapist usually assists persons to enter alternative territories of their lives through gateways of the present - "unique outcomes" to those readers who are familiar with my writings. When family members are encouraged to respond to these unique outcomes as one might respond to a mystery, they suddenly discover many previously neglected experiences of the past "resonating" with these unique outcomes. These experiences, that would not under ordinary circumstances be remembered, "light up" and contribute to alternative story lines. There seem to be twin "constructive" processes at work here: generation and resurrection. The generative part relates very much to the triggering of imagination, and I believe that some of the questions and languages of therapy in re-authoring practices are essential to this. Perhaps we could say that they trigger "reverberations".

Andrew: What does all this mean for therapy?

Michael: For me, it suggests that further investigation of the source of imagination and reverie in this work is in order. David Epston and I have often discussed the picturesque nature of the language of this therapy, and

Bachelard's ideas just might assist in the exploration of, and extension of, the limits of this work.

Andrew: In a way, you're describing the imagination as a source of the new.

Michael: Yes, I am. But also as a source of the previously neglected or unremembered "old" via these resonances.

Andrew: Can we go back to the issue of training. How is your current thinking reflected in your training practices?

Michael: Just as I am interested in structuring therapy as a context for the re-authoring of lives, I am interested in training as a re-authoring context.

Andrew: So you pay particular attention to the experiences and beliefs of the person in training?

Michael. Yes. There are a number of exercises that I have been experimenting with in training that encourage participants to identify which aspects of their lived experience are being expressed in this work, and that assist participants to determine more clearly their preferred beliefs in relation to this work. For example, sometimes I interview participants about the history of their presence in the training courses at Dulwich Centre. I am interested to find what it was that attracted them to the training course. What is it about this story of therapy that provides the frame for training, that prompted their application? How does this fit with their own preferred values and practices? What is the history of these preferences in their lives and in their careers? What were the particular events or experiences that helped them to determine these preferences? Did any of these events constitute turning points for them? How did reflection on these events assist them to work out what they believed to be important for their work, to work out what they would stand by? And so on. These and other "re-authoring" exercises encourage participants to become familiar with the unique nature of their expression of this work - if you like, to become more aware of their preferred style, and to be more aware of the extent to which they are actually "originating" through this expression. As participants become more familiar with these exercises, they can engage each other in them.

Andrew: So, just as your therapy enables families to draw on experiences that may otherwise be lost, your training invites those who are training to notice and value experiences of their own that might otherwise be lost?

Michael: Yes, it's a parallel process. And it enables participants to experience this work first-hand. It helps them to appreciate the multi-storied nature of life, and has real effects on the course of their own lives.

Andrew: At the recent national conference in Adelaide, Maria Scicchitano made the point in her workshop that much of family therapy training, until recently, has been founded on the view that trainees would have to "unlearn" ideas and theories they value that are perhaps not consistent with a family systems view. It sounds like you are advocating a greater respect of the trainee and what they bring with them as people.

Michael: I am advocating that position. However, I don't see it as useful for training to become a "free-for-all". I do believe that it is often necessary to assist participants to deconstruct, and thereby challenge, certain ideas and theories that they bring to the training context. For example, normative and totalising ideas about the shape of family life, and the so-called "truth" theories of the psychotherapies. But this deconstruction is not difficult, as the therapy and training itself resembles deconstructive method.

And I certainly make it clear that I have little interest in joining with participants around practices that are informed by the more positivist models - there are other places that participants can go to do that.

Andrew: Can we talk briefly about research. Does it interest you?

Michael: I agree with Karl Tomm's opinion that those people who are practicing therapy, along with the persons who seek therapy, are the primary or basic researchers, and that those people who collect data in a more formal way are the secondary or supportive researchers. I've always been interested in primary research, and find the continual demands from secondary researchers that primary researchers justify their existence to be quite tedious.

If the secondary researchers in our field could go further in relinquishing the moral high ground, and in revisioning research along the lines of recent developments in ethnomethodology - which would include the rendering transparent of the socially-constructed nature of their enterprise - then what secondary researchers do might become more relevant to what primary researchers do. I am sure that they could then have a very enriching collaboration. In saying this, I don't want to totalise secondary research. There are already some very sparkling developments in secondary research in this field.

Andrew: I'd like to ask you about the way we name our practice. Some critics argue that our choice of the term "family therapy" has become outdated and should be changed in some way to include the broader field. What is your thought on that?

Michael: For me, it's what the term "family therapy" symbolises that counts - its historical associations, its situation in the social field of the psychotherapies, its domain of possible activities, and so on. I believe family therapy has signified a field that has, at times, been radically open and pluralistic. It has been possible, in this field, at different points in history, for persons to stretch the limits of what it is possible to think at those particular points. In my view it is still open, and still pluralistic, and I think that this is perhaps its most important strength. Family therapy does not signify a "closed shop".

However, despite this, I do appreciate the fact that family therapy has historically supported some practices that would now be viewed as subjugating. There also is a considerable danger that family therapy could become thoroughly institutionalised. And this is where the importance of a spirit of critique comes to the fore.

Andrew: You mentioned a spirit of critique. There was certainly a sense of that at the recent conference in Adelaide.

Michael: Yes, I sensed this too. It was a very good conference. In my view, it continued the trend set by the Christchurch conference of a couple of years ago.

Andrew: How did you experience these conferences as different?

Michael: ·I think people are struggling with the pressing issues more, such as racism, power practices in therapy, and so on. It seems to me we are having a higher regard for moral and ethical responsibilities, rather than for techniques or packages.

Andrew: You've been actively involved in the family therapy field for a long time now. In what ways do you experience present-day family therapy as different from how it was when you first became involved?

Michael: It's certainly very different. The most striking difference is that there is now a strong family therapy network, and that the practices of family therapy are generally well-accepted now in many institutions and agencies. Twenty years ago, in Adelaide, the practices associated with family therapy were not so well tolerated, and at times it was something of a struggle for those who were enthusiastic about it to persist with these practices. Of course, there are still politics surrounding the practices of family therapy, and I expect there always will be, but I am sure there are many more opportunities for persons in this field now.

Andrew: Does family therapy excite you as much as it did in the beginning?

Michael: Probably more so. I think there are some fantastic developments in this field. I am in touch with many therapists whose creative contributions are having something of a transformative effect on the field. And it appears to me that today's younger generation of family therapists are less "captured" by the so-called schools of family therapy. It goes without saying that this is a good thing.

Andrew: The concept of creativity is never far from therapists' minds. What helps you to stay creative and at the cutting edge?

Michael: That's difficult for me to answer. Not having to worry about the bureaucratic and organisational restraints that are a feature of a great number of institutions and agencies certainly helps. Viewing my work as ongoing private research also helps. Part of this includes consulting families about their experience of therapy, and this is always invigorating.

Andrew: So it's a constant spirit of enquiry and investigation.

Michael: Yes, there is such a lot to learn and discover.

Andrew: Michael, if you could predict the future, where do you see family therapy in ten or twenty years?

Michael: I wouldn't care to attempt to predict the future of family therapy. However, there are a number of things that I would like to see happen in the field. For example, I would like to see an increased tolerance of difference. Coupled to this is my hope that Australian family therapists will further challenge the philosophy behind the "tall poppy" syndrome. This syndrome is accompanied by cultural practices that have a negative and discouraging effect on those persons who are perceived to be in a certain position in family therapy in Australia, and it also has a negative and discouraging effect on those who are not perceived to be in these positions. These persons are not inspired to articulate and present unique developments in their own work in contexts where this will gain the recognition it deserves.

I would also like to see the family therapy community developing more ways of supporting and encouraging Australian and New Zealand therapists to visit family therapy centres in other countries. Cheryl White, of Dulwich Centre Publications, has put together some scholarships that achieve this very purpose, and I think it would be a very positive thing if other centres and associations found ways of taking up and extending this sort of development.

And I would like to see an extension of those developments which relate to the exploration of men's experience of men's culture, and to the addressing of the complex social justice issues, including those that relate to gender, race, poverty, and so on.

Andrew: Perhaps what you are proposing would be liberating for therapists too.

Michael: Yes, I agree.

REFERENCES

Hoffman, L. 1990:
"Constructing realities: An art of lenses." **Family Process,** 29(1):1-12.
South Australian Film Corporation, 1976:
"They reckon a woman's world's just it and a bit." Penny Chapman, Producer; Meg Stewart, Director.
Waldegrave, C. 1990:
"Just Therapy." **Dulwich Centre Newsletter,** 1:5-46. (A special issue on social justice and family therapy, a discussion of the work of The Family Centre, Lower Hutt, New Zealand.)
Wood, A. 1990:
"The consumer's view of the team and the one-way screen: A preliminary investigation." **Dulwich Centre Newsletter,** 2:21-23.

4. Naming Abuse and Breaking From its Effects*

*Interviewer: Christopher McLean***

Chris: Your approach to working with survivors of abuse seems to focus on helping people to break free of the negative stories they hold about themselves. Could you start by talking about this?

Michael: When I meet with a person who has survived abuse in childhood and adolescence, very often what's brought them to the consultation are certain behaviours that are self-destructive or self-abusive, behaviours that are experienced as actions against the self, that are unfavourable to their life. These actions can take many forms including self-mutilation, addictions, and multiple suicide attempts. It is my view that these self-destructive behaviours are an expression of the abuse that the person has been subject to. But this is a particular form of the expression of this experience. This is an expression of the experience of abuse that brings about profoundly negative consequences in the person's life, an expression of the abuse that informs real effects that are highly impoverishing to the person's life.

---

* This interview was conducted at Dulwich Centre in May 1994.

** Christopher McLean can be contacted c/- Dulwich Centre Publications.

The narrative metaphor provides a particular perspective on this phenomenon. It would suggest that these self-destructive expressions of the abuse are shaped by the meanings that the person is giving to the abuse itself; that it is these meanings that determine the form of the expression of one's experiences in life. This consideration is usually confirmed when we talk with people about their understandings of the abuse that they have been subject to. These understandings invariably feature themes of culpability and unworthiness; that somehow the person deserved the abuse or had it coming to them, or could have stopped it if they really wanted to. And, in that these people believe that the acts of self-abuse confirm these themes, there is a circularity to all of this.

To summarise, self-abuse is an expression of one's experiences of abuse, an expression that is shaped by the meanings given to the abuse. And the shape of this expression, in turn confirms these meanings. It is the meanings that mediate the expression of one's experience of abuse. So when we are considering the nature of people's expressions of abuse, it is vitally important that we consider these expressions as units of experience and meaning.

Chris: How are these meanings arrived at?

Michael: These meanings are arrived at very much through the private stories that people have about their lives. These stories provide the frame through which people interpret their experiences of life. And if a person is recruited into a very negative story about who they are as a person, then it is likely that they will give meanings to their experiences that emphasise culpability and worthlessness.

Chris: So where does that take you in terms of working with people who have survived abuse and who have been recruited into very negative stories about who they are, and who might be expressing their experience of abuse in ways that are self-abusive and self-destructive?

Michael: It suggests that one of the primary tasks of this work is to assist these people to derive alternative meanings of their experiences of abuse; to establish the conditions that make it possible for them to reinterpret the abuse. If we can play some part in assisting these people to break their lives from those very negative personal stories that have such a profound effect on shaping the expression of their experience, and if we can help them to step into some other more positive account of who they might be as a person, then it will become possible for them to actively engage in the reinterpretation of the abuse that they were subject to. And this reinterpretation will change the shape of the expression of people's experiences of abuse, and therefore the shape of their lives.

Chris: Say something more about the process of this reinterpretation.

Michael: This reinterpretation is not one that is imposed by the therapist, but one that is generated collaboratively in the course of this work. When people break their lives from the very negative stories of their identity, and when they have the opportunity to stand in a different territory of their life, they start interpreting their experiences of abuse as exploitation, as tyranny, as torture, as violence and so on. It's very clear that this reinterpretation facilitates a different expression of their experience of abuse. This expression of the abuse now takes the form of outrage, of passion for justice, of acts to address injustice, of testimony, of searching out contexts in which others might be available to bear witness to these testimonies, and so on.

These alternative forms of expression of a person's experiences of abuse are not lesser expressions of one's experiences of abuse than those self-destructive forms. As expressions of one's experiences of abuse, these are not less complete. In fact, the people with whom I work invariably state that these alternative forms constitute a fuller expression of that experience. These are expressions of that experience that brings with them very different real effects on the shape of their lives, effects that are judged to be constructive rather than destructive.

Chris: I believe that you have some reservations about practices involving revisiting the original traumatic experience as a way of breaking free of it. I would be interested if you could explain your concerns, as it seems to relate to what you have been saying.

Michael: First things first. There is no excuse for people to experience re-traumatisation within the context of therapy. Distress yes, re-traumatisation no. I believe that the notion of healing practices based on the imperative of returning to the site of the abuse in order to re-experience this is a highly questionable notion, and, as well, dangerous. This notion is often justified by the theory of catharsis, and this is a theory that obscures the critical dimension of meaning. To simply encourage people to return to the site of trauma can reinforce for them the dominant meanings that inform the self-destructive expression of the experience of abuse. And, this can contribute to renewed trauma and it can incite renewed actions of self-abuse.

Of course, there are many other reasons to question this idea about the importance of returning to the site of trauma. At the time that these people were subject to abuse, they had no power, they had no choice - they were trapped. In response to such impossible and agonising circumstances, many developed rather fantastic mechanisms that enabled them to escape the abusive context - not materially, but to spirit themselves away in mind. Others used what little manoeuvering space that was available to them to create experiences of self-sustenance - and, in circumstances such as these, this is simply an extraordinary achievement. Now let me pose a question. In requiring people to return to the site of trauma, are we not reproducing conditions that are entrapping, that are dispossessing people of choice?

And there are other questions that we could ask about this. In requiring people to return to the site of trauma, are we not also unwittingly reproducing our culture's phobia about flight? Are we not being just too complicit with this culture's imperative of "facing up"? And in this complicity, are we not closing down the possibilities that might be available to people for the honouring of the special skills and the personal qualities that made it possible for them to navigate through the dark hours of their lives and into the present?

Chris: What is the alternative?

Michael: In the work that I am proposing, it does become possible for people to give expression to their experience of abuse in ways that don't bring about the negative consequences to which I have referred. Circumstances can be established that make it possible for people to enter their lives into alternative expressions of their experience, and this can be achieved without imposition on the therapist's part. Under these circumstances, people find themselves standing in some of the alternative territories of their lives, territories in which they can get in touch with different and more positive stories of their identity. And this makes it possible for people to give different meanings to their experiences of abuse which, in turn, makes it possible for them to express these experiences in ways that aren't likely to be retraumatising of them.

Chris: I think that the whole concept of the cathartic expression of grief as a freeing thing is so deeply ingrained in modern ways of thinking about these sorts of issues, that what you're saying could easily sound as though you favour a very intellectual way of dealing with the effects of abuse, and that somehow you are uncomfortable with the open expression of emotion. I wonder if you would like to say a bit about that.

Michael: I cry with the people who consult me, and I also laugh with them. I join them in outrage, and also in joy. We experience sadness together, and also hope. As I walk for a while with these people, I experience all of the emotions that one experiences in bearing witness to testimony. As well, there are contexts in which I find myself celebrating with people - contexts in which the alternative stories of their lives are being honoured, when the other accounts of their identity are being powerfully authenticated. And I experience inspiration from the steps that people take to dispossess perpetrators of their authority, the steps that people take in reclaiming the territories of their lives, in the refashioning of their lives, in having the "last say" about who they are.

So, let me put to rest these concerns about "intellectual ways" and about "discomfort with emotion". I do not regard my position to be an academic or an intellectual one. But this doesn't mean that I feel compelled to join the dominant "feeling discourse" of the culture of psychotherapy, to practice in the ways that are specified by this discourse, and to talk with people about the experiences of their lives in the contemporary ways of speaking about such things that are prescribed in and sanctioned by this discourse. I do not respond at all well to the various incitements to "fit myself out" with the responses that are called for by this "feeling discourse".

At this point, I would like to further respond to your comment by reiterating what I have said about the notion of catharsis. I don't believe that there is any expression of any experience that stands outside a system of meaning. And I would also like to reiterate what I have said about distress. There is an entirely significant distinction to be drawn between distress and traumatisation. I think it is possible for people to be expressing aspects of their experiences of abuse in ways that might be distressing, but that aren't re-traumatising of them. It is possible and desirable for people to find options for giving voice to their experiences of abuse in ways that are profoundly healing for them, and in ways that they judge to be entirely expressive.

Chris: How can you be sure that re-traumatisation is not occurring?

Michael: We can assist people to take a far more active role in monitoring the real effects of the expressions of their experiences of abuse, instead of leaving it to chance or to the authority of a therapist. Very often, when people attend therapy, they get disconnected from this role. They cease to monitor the consequences of their interactions with their therapist, and leave this to the therapist's determination. This outcome is problematic. Throughout the process of therapy, we need to be continually consulting people about what they perceive to be the effects of our work with them, about how the reinterpretation and expression of their experience is affecting the shape of their lives, and about what they understand to be the limitations and possibilities associated with our conversations.

Chris: I'd like now to explore your views on the importance of establishing a political or contextual appreciation of a person's experience of abuse, and, in particular, how the concept of recruitment fits into this idea.

Michael: To assist people to establish an account of the politics of their experience helps to undermine the self-blame and the shame that is so often experienced in relation to the abuse itself. One way that this can be achieved is through engaging with people in externalizing conversations about the self-hate, self-loathing, or whatever it is that constitutes the person's primary relationship with their "self". In these externalizing conversations, we can explore with people what this self-hate talks them into about who they are as people, how it has them treating their lives, their bodies, their thoughts, how it interferes in their relationships with others, and so on. And together we can also explore the processes by which the person was recruited into self-hate and self-loathing.

Chris: So you emphasise questions about how the person got recruited into self-hate, or self-loathing, or whatever, and this has the effect of bringing forth the politics of the person's experience?

Michael: Yes, it is primarily through such questions that this is achieved. It is through such questions that we wind up identifying the specifics of this process of recruitment - not just the physical processes of abuse, but also the knowledges, the strategies and the techniques that were employed, and the workings of these knowledges, strategies and techniques. But we would not arrive at this place by referencing our work to the idea of returning to the site of the trauma. In responding to these externalizing questions, people are actually engaging in a reinterpretation of their experiences of abuse, and are breaking from the negative stories of identity that have been so capturing of them. No longer can the abuse reflect personal culpability, and no longer does it reflect to people the truth of their "nature" and of their "personality". I believe that these externalizing conversations can be considered as "deconstructing" conversations.

Perhaps another way of stating this, one that is inspired by the

---

narrative metaphor, is that the reinterpretation that is triggered by these questions provides a basis for a renaming of the dominant plots of people's lives - away from themes of personal culpability, and towards exploitation, tyranny, abuse, and so on.

Chris: You have talked, I believe, about the importance of naming abuse, not simply as abuse, but in its particularities. Could you say more about that?

Michael: Yes. I understand that it is really important that people go further than a general naming of the abuse. The word abuse is an important but global term, but its lack of specificity is somewhat limiting in several senses. For example, testimony requires specificity, as does the establishment of a capacity to discern, in one's life, actions that are of a loving nature from actions that are abusive or exploitative. Also, to connect one's experiences of abuse to the dominant knowledges and practices of power in our culture requires this specificity.

Once abuse knowledges and techniques are established in their specificity, they can be contextualised - linked to the dominant knowledges and practices of power of our culture, the familiar operations of which can be traced through history in families and other institutions of our culture, and through the history of the dominant knowledges and practices of men's ways of being in relation to women, children, and to other men. This contextualisation of abuse knowledges and practices is a very important aspect of this work. It provides further opportunities for the reinterpretation of one's experiences of abuse and for the deconstruction of the negative stories of identity of which we have been speaking.

Once abuse knowledges and practices are established in their specificity, this very significantly (a) facilitates the preparation of "adequate" testimony, one that is experience-near, (b) assists people to develop a degree of "discernment" that makes it possible for them to distinguish those actions that are directed towards them that are exploitative, abusive or neglectful in nature from those actions directed towards them that are supportive, loving or caring in nature, and (c) expands the possibilities that are before people to take action to resist and to challenge these knowledges and practices in their day-to-day lives.

Chris: I believe that you have, on occasion, even prescribed the reading of a book on the purposes and effects of torture. I am wondering about what actual effects this has, and, in the light of your statements about re-traumatisation, is there a danger that this could in actual fact be a traumatising experience?

Michael: I'd like to go back to the point that I was making before about meaning. I'd never suggest such reading until I had a strong sense that the person who was consulting me was actually engaging in the reinterpretation of their experiences of abuse. Once that's established, it can be very helpful to read such accounts. It is particularly interesting to people who have survived abuse to learn that those people who have survived torture also experienced similar degrees of guilt and shame, and were recruited into very negative attitudes towards themselves through that experience. It might be distressing to read of these accounts under these circumstances, but the transparency is not re-traumatising. This contributes further to the renaming of the abuse.

It really helps for people to know that torture is not a test that establishes an individual's moral worth, that torture is not a response to wrong-doing, that torture is not even primarily about extracting confessions - but that its purposes relate more to breaking down identity, to breaking down a sense of community and to isolating people from each other, to destroying self-respect and to demoralising, to depersonalising the world in people's experience of it, and so on. For those who have survived abuse, this is an important understanding, one that undermines the sense of culpability and of shame that is so disabling.

Chris: You have talked about the importance of survivors of abuse expressing outrage at what they have experienced. How do you think this is affected by our culture's attitude to anger, particularly women's anger?

Michael: I do appreciate that everybody has the right to express what is generally referred to as anger, and the fact that for women this right has so often been disqualified in this culture. But I do want to ask, "Why this word?" Why always mediate this expression through a word like anger? In this culture, people always want to talk about anger, and they do so within the context of a specific discourse. In the context of this discourse, anger is so highly valued. It's venerated. It is put on a pedestal. It is constantly referred to. It is considered the primary force of our nature. It is fetishised. This anger is something that people are always having to do something about. We are fixated on the notion of "unresolved anger". It is considered to be at the root of all sorts of terrible maladies. But I've often thought that perhaps this fixation itself is the malady that we suffer from.

And there is so much talk about "the angry woman", which is invariably a disqualification of women's experience of gender politics. I have often been consulted by women who refer to themselves in this way and who have learned to pathologise themselves on this account. I have interviewed these women about how they have made this interpretation, and they often share with me the "insights" that they have achieved during previous counselling experiences. Now, these insights provide for thinking about whatever the experience of "anger" is in a way that is devoid of context. Anger, in this sense, is one of those words that is part of a discourse that psychologises, obscures context, and limits possibilities for action in the world. But what about "outrage"? What about "passion" for justice? These interpretations or descriptions are part of a different discourse, one that brings with it options for addressing context, and options for the expression of this experience through action. Discourses are constitutive, they are shaping of our lives. Within the context of these alternative interpretations or descriptions, the experience that is so often referred to as anger is no longer something to be worked through, or some state of being, but something to be honoured.

Chris: What you are saying here about anger seems to me to fit in with some of the concerns that I have heard you express about popular psychological concepts as co-dependency, and about systems analyses that interpret abuse as a function of a relationship. Could you say more about your concerns?

Michael: All of this psychologising of personal experience, and all of these formal analyses, are deeply conservative. They are invariably pathologising of the lives of those people who have been subject to abuse, and, in so doing, divert attention from the politics of the situation. As well, so many of the interpretations of this sort discriminate against women's ways of being in the world and champion dominant men's ways of being in the world.

Chris: One of the specific notions implicated in this is the idea that women who have experienced abuse actively seek further abusive relationships due to some internalized, psychological mechanisms. Could you comment on this?

Michael: This is an interpretation that is based on certain observations. Women who have experienced abuse in childhood and adolescence, and who have, in their adult life, stepped into a relationship in which a man has subjected them to further abuse, often only escape these relationships to wind up in other relationships in which they are again subject to abuse by men. This phenomenon is taken up into the various psychologies, and triggers the fabrication of a whole range of explanations that refer to psychological mechanisms. Most of these explanations include a pathological account of the woman's motive for entering into these relationships.

Now, we have to ask, what effects do these interpretations have on women's lives? Well, I have asked women this question, and I am sure that it would not be too hard for you to guess the responses that have come back. These interpretations encourage women to take responsibility for the abuse that is being perpetrated by men. These interpretations encourage women to persevere in relationships in which they are being subject to violence by men. Interpretations of this sort are in the service of maintaining the status quo.

Chris: So, how else might this phenomenon be interpreted - women who have been subject to abuse entering into relationships in which they are further abused by men?

Michael: There is lots of evidence to support the idea that this vulnerability is born of difficulties in the area of discernment - difficulties in distinguishing abuse from nurture, neglect from care, exploitation from love, and so on. This difficulty with discernment renders many women quite vulnerable to being exploited in relationships. If it is not possible for a woman to discern abuse from nurture at the outset of a relationship, then it is not possible for her to attend to the early warning signs and to confront this abuse, and to seize upon the option of breaking the connection before it becomes more fully established and encompassing of her identity.

Chris: What's the background for this difficulty in discernment, with this difficulty in drawing crucial distinctions around one's experience?

Michael: Most people who have been abused as children or adolescents have experienced this within the institutions of our culture that are formally designated as loving and caring contexts - that is, in families, extended kinship networks, or in the institutions that substitute for families and for these networks. To experience abuse in contexts that are designated as loving and caring contexts is both mystifying and confusing. To experience abuse in these contexts makes it difficult for people to establish the distinctions to which I have referred, that is those that relate to abuse and nurture, neglect and care, exploitation and love. The popular myth that the family is "the haven in a cruel world" has contributed significantly to this mystification. It has been established that a very significant proportion of families are highly dangerous places for children.

But we don't need to experience abuse in our families of origin to have later difficulties in discerning abuse from nurture. At times we all find it difficult to make this discernment. After all, we have grown up in a culture that is informed by folklore that blurs crucial distinctions: "You've got to be cruel to be kind", "Spare the rod, spoil the child", and so on. Now, for those people who have been subject to abuse, and I am here talking about traumatic abuse perpetrated in a context that this culture defines as protective and supportive, this makes it incredibly more difficult to discern abuse from nurture and exploitation from love.

And, for many, this blurring of significant distinctions is recurrent. Let us take commonly-accepted notions of jealousy. So often counsellors are consulted by women who are subject to forms of abuse from their male partners that are interpreted as "jealousy". And, in these circumstances, this display of "jealousy" is understood to be an indicator of the extent to which the man values the woman partner, or is taken as a reflection of the degree of the intensity of his feelings for her. Women who have been subject to abuse historically are highly vulnerable to these sorts of interpretations that are used by men justify and extend on their abusive behaviours.

Chris: Could you say something about how you go about reinterpreting these stories, so that a person who has experienced abuse is more able to develop this capacity for discernment?

Michael: Therapy can provide a context for assisting people to establish this discernment. We can start by exploring with them some of the real effects of the abuses that they have been subject to in their lives. We can work to identify self-destructive acts as expressions of experiences of abuse, and we can engage them in conversations that draw distinctions around these sorts of expressions of the experience of abuse and those sort of expressions that are based on a reinterpretation or a renaming of the abuse itself. We can work together to identify unique outcomes - those personal actions that cannot be read as self-rejection, but as self-care. These unique outcomes provide a point of entry to the counterplots of women's lives, those accounts that have to do with survival, resilience, protest, resistance, and so on.

Once these plots have been juxtaposed, and as this work proceeds, we can encourage the woman to sort their day-to-day experiences of life into one or the other. Does this event fit with abuse or self-abuse, or does it fit with care or self-care? Does this interaction invite self-rejection, or does it invite self-acceptance? And so on. One outcome of this work is that it becomes much easier for women to distinguish the different actions that they are subject to, and those that they subject themselves to, as either supportive or neglectful of their person. Another outcome is that the counterplots of women's lives become more clearly articulated - this sorting and linking process "thickens" these counterplots - and often for the first time women begin to identify preferred accounts of their wants, tastes, desires, purposes, goals, hopes and so on.

As this capacity, this skill in discernment develops, women report that the confusion that has been all-pervasive begins to dissipate. Women and men who have been subject to abuse in childhood and adolescence, and who have been isolated in this abuse, so often report that they never experience being in touch with life. And more than this. Not only do they talk of their inability to touch life, but also of the fact that they cannot see "it" clearly - that trying to see life is like looking through a haze or a fog. As people start to draw the sort of distinctions to which I have been referring, invariably the fog begins to lift. Initially there are wonderful but fleeting episodes of clarity of "sight". Over time, this clarity is generalised. Women are then less at risk of persisting in relationships in which they are subject to abuse and exploitation.

Chris: So often during the course of this interview, you have emphasised the importance of bringing forth the context of people's experiences of abuse. I did have some understanding of this before this interview, but it has to an extent surprised me to hear about just how far you go in attending to context in this work.

Michael: You are right about this emphasis. It is very important that the abusive practices to which men and women are subject get put in context. This is important for all of the reasons that we have already discussed, and also because it brings for the people who consult us an appreciation of the extent to which they are not the sole recipients of these abusive practices, that this is not something that is unique to their lives - that, although the abuse was isolating of them from others, they were not alone in their experience of this.

I know that people can achieve this appreciation without in anyway contributing to an understatement of their experience of the trauma of abuse - without in any way minimising this experience, or the expression of this experience - and without in any way diminishing their understanding of and articulation of the very significant consequences of this abuse to their lives. As people reference their experiences of abuse to context, they become less vulnerable to the pathologising of their identities, and less likely to be recruited into the shame that this pathologising is in league with.

An understanding of this context also makes it possible for people to determine the extent to which their own parents might have been reproducing the abusive practices that they were subject to in their own families of origin, and to determine whether or not their parents had done even fractionally better than their grandparents did. Of course, not all parents do better than their parents did, and some do worse. But women and men have informed me that determinations of this sort are very important. Determinations of this sort engage people in a comprehension of the extent to which, in their personal work to reclaim their lives from the effects of abuse, they are involved in a project that has to do with making it their business to challenge abusive practices that have often been carried across generations in their families. And determinations of this sort make it possible for these women and men to appreciate the ways that they might have done better than their own parents did, and provides them with direction in the furthering of this work.

Chris: For some reason, this discussion brings to mind a question that I have heard you use in your work: "If you'd had yourself for a parent, what difference would this have made to your life?" This raised my curiosity. What are you getting at with this question?

Michael: There are two categories of questions of this sort that are very helpful, and they go something like this:

(a) *How do you imagine your life might have been if you'd had yourself as a father/mother? If you'd had yourself for a mother/father, what would have been appreciated about you as a child that wasn't appreciated in you as a child? What difference would it have made to you growing up if you'd had yourself for a father/mother? In what ways would you have been more accepting of yourself? In what ways do you think that you might have experienced yourself as lovable?*

(b) *Just imagine, if you were your own son/daughter, what would it be about your experience of being parented that would enrich your life? If you were your own son/daughter, what parenting qualities do you think you would be experiencing that would be enriching of your life?*

Questions of this sort are generally effective in challenging the negative "truths" of identity that people get recruited into through their experiences of abuse. One's sense of identity is very significantly determined by one's experience of other people's experiences of who one is. And since one's parents are primary in this, so often it is parents who abuse who wind up having the last say about who one is, and about how one relates to one's self. Questions of the sort that I have outlined here undermine the authority of parents who abuse, who are mostly men, and open up possibilities for women and men to revise their relationship with their "self".

These questions make it possible for people to identify aspects of their lives as children, as well as personal qualities and characteristics, that might have been entirely appreciated under other circumstances, within the contexts of other relationships. These questions also make it possible for people who have been abused to experience the sort of compassion for themselves that they often experience for others. In this way, women and men's responses to these questions have the effect of dispossessing those parents who abuse from having the last say on matters of identity.

Chris: Okay, that satisfies my curiosity to an extent. But I would like to know more about this, so perhaps we could pick it up again at some other time. Let us now turn to the difficulties that women have in leaving and staying out of relationships in which men are abusing them. I know that you have said that this can be far more difficult than most women expect.

Michael: There are many important considerations that make it difficult for women to leave these relationships. Apart from those that we have already discussed in this interview, there are considerations of an economic nature, and those that relate to the existence of few options for alternative housing, lack of support from relatives and friends, threats and harassment from the men concerned, and so on.

But there is another important consideration that we should discuss here. Usually, at the point of separation, and/or in the period leading up . to this point, women who are being abused by their men partners do experience rising expectations - expectations that, through this course of action, that is, separation, they might emerge from the terror and the despair that has become so much part of their daily existence, and expectations that they might find themselves arriving at a degree of well-being. However, despite the rising expectations that are experienced up to the point of separation and for a short time after this, wherever these women find themselves following separation - whether this be in their own accommodation, in refuges or staying with friends or relatives - there is a very real risk early in this journey that they will turn back to an unchanged violent situation. And, a great percentage of women in fact do this.

So often, shortly after leaving the man who is violent, women begin to lose their sense of relief at having escaped, as well as their hopefulness about new options and possibilities for their own lives and for the lives of their children, and find themselves sinking back into despair. Very soon they find themselves in a "trough", one characterised by confusion, disorientation, profound insecurity, and a sense of personal failure. Women's experience of this trough can be so overwhelming that they can find themselves feeling even worse than they did prior to leaving the abusive man. This development is often read as regress ("I am worse off than before"), and for many women this reading plays a significant role in forming a decision to turn back to an unchanged violent situation, despite the alarm and the protest that this decision arouses in concerned others.

However, other readings of this "trough-like" experience are available, and some of these bring interpretations of this that can contribute significantly to averting this turning back to an unchanged violent situation, and can introduce new possibilities for action that are likely to be supportive of, and sustaining of, women through the separation process.

Chris: What is an example of such an alternative interpretation, and how is this introduced?

Michael: If women who are working to leave and to stay out of relationships in which they are subject to violence by men appreciate the extent to which this project engages them in a "migration of identity", and if they come to understand the processes involved in such migrations, then it becomes more possible for them to see this project through.

The identity that women have experienced prior to the separation is one that has been imposed in so many ways by the man who is abusive of them, and, as well, by other persons who might have perpetrated abuse in their families of origins, and/or in some of the other institutions of this culture.

Because achieving control of the woman is such an imperative for men who abuse, throughout their relationships with women they go about relentlessly and systematically reinterpreting these women's histories and identities. So, when women take steps to break free, they are doing a great deal more than breaking from the ongoing trauma, they are doing a great deal more than breaking from a familiar social network, and they are doing a great deal more than stepping into material insecurity - although all of this alone is more than enough to have to deal with at any time in one's life.

At this time, women are also embarking on a migration of identity. And, in this migration, there is always some distance between the point of separation from the abusive context and the point of arrival at some preferred location in life, and at some alternative and preferred account of one's identity. There is always some distance between these two points in terms of time. And in this space, as in any migratory process, women characteristically go through a range of experiences, many of them difficult. In this "liminal" or "betwixt and between" space, confusion and disorientation reigns, and often nothing seems manageable any more, not even one's relationship with one's children. It is in this space that women are vulnerable to a sense of total incompetence and personal failure, to feelings of desperation and acute despair.

Chris: So, how is this migration metaphor helpful in this work?

Michael: If women have the opportunity to map their experience of the descent into this trough of confusion and disorientation as part of a process, if they have the opportunity to map this as a part of an ongoing journey, rather than interpret it as regress, then they are less at risk of turning back to an unchanged violent context. If women can understand these experiences as the products of a migration of identity, it becomes more possible for them to persevere with their journey despite the disorientation and the confusion. Such acts of mapping assist women to place their distress within the context of progress, to stand by and to hold onto the idea that the future might hold something different for them, to hold onto their hopes, to their expectations for a better life, to keep in sight the horizon of another world.

To facilitate this mapping of one's experience of these migrations of identity, I regularly share with the women who consult me the graphs of other women's migration experiences under similar circumstances - graphs that other women have put together during our work, graphs that these women have given me permission to share with others. Upon reviewing these graphs, I regularly encourage the women who are consulting me to mark where they think they might be in their journey.

Chris: So women are invited to plot their own journey through reference to the journey of others?

Michael: Yes. I encourage women to reflect on their experiences of this migration, to choose one of the sample graphs, and to mark on this the point at which they believe they are currently located in this journey. Women find that to put a cross on a graph that provides them with some indication of their location in a trajectory called a "migration of identity" - the very act of doing this - brings about a dramatic change in their attitude towards what they are going through. Interpretations of regress dissolve, and hope, an antidote to despair, resurfaces - and this is something that women can rely upon to see themselves through all of the confusion and disorientation that characterises, and can be predicted for, such journeys.

Chris: How do you go about introducing the idea of marking one's location on these maps?

Michael: I usually ask questions like: *This is where Jane was at the three week mark. You are three weeks into this. Where do you think you are on this graph? Where would you locate your present position?* Mary might respond to these questions with something like, "Well, I think I'm feeling worse than Jane was at this point", and, depending on the shape of the sample graph, might wind up placing a mark on the graph that locates her current position somewhere further into the journey. Or Mary might say, "I don't think I'm feeling quite as desperate as Jane was at this point, so I think I'm here", and might locate her current position at a point that Jane had already reached at two weeks into her migration. I will include a copy of one of these graphs that might be published along with this transcript [page 102]. From this, readers will see that, in the initial stage of this migration, because of the sorts of experiences that can be predicted in migrations of identity, feeling worse is invariably interpreted as progress rather than regress.

Chris: So, women breaking from violent contexts are less at risk for turning back when they can refer to these maps. And if they can read their experience within the context of these maps they will know what to expect?

Michael: Yes. And in this way begin to feel less alarmed about the "betwixt

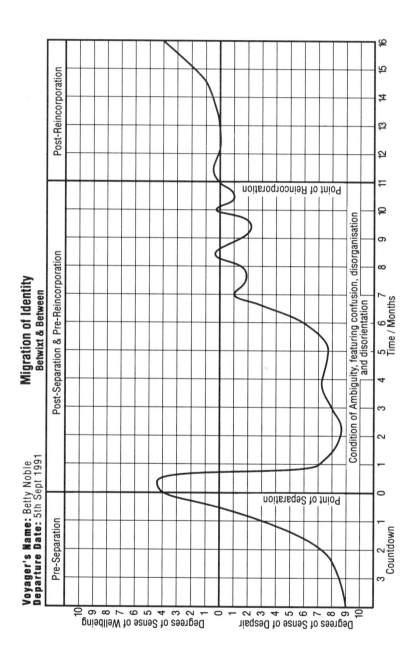

Migration of Identity
Betwixt & Between

Voyager's Name: Betty Noble
Departure Date: 5th Sept 1991

Pre-Separation

Post-Separation & Pre-Reincorporation

Post-Reincorporation

Point of Separation

Point of Reincorporation

Condition of Ambiguity, featuring confusion, disorganisation and disorientation

Degrees of Sense of Wellbeing

Degrees of Sense of Despair

Time / Months

Countdown

and between" experiences of confusion, disorientation, and so on, and less vulnerable to states of acute despair which can only be complicating to these journeys.

I would like to emphasise here that no two graphs of this migration of identity are exactly alike, and together we have the task of identifying the particularities of the woman's journey. To achieve this, we can spend time reviewing all that the woman is separating from, as well as her recent experiences of the journey, and can begin speculating about what this might suggest about the future - about future circumstances of life, about ways of being in the world that might be on the horizon. We can also step into speculation about the distance that might be expected between separation and arrival or "reincorporation".

To assist speculation, I often share with women some of the details of the journeys of other women who had similar graphs. Based on the understandings of these journeys that other women have given me, I usually inform women that the very minimum time required for these migrations of identity is about nine months. However, I also inform them that, if the circumstances of this journey are right, they can expect to be feeling somewhat better well in advance of the point at which they are established in another location of life, and at a point at which they have secured a different and preferred sense of identity.

Chris: What do you mean, "if the circumstances are right?"

Michael: We can work to establish the right circumstances. For example, I usually encourage the women who consult me to interview other women about their migrations. These might be migrations similar to their own, or other kinds of migrations, including geographical migrations. In Australia, there would be very few people who would not know anyone who has migrated, and most would know someone who found the migration process difficult - who found the going hard to the extent that they nearly turned back, or perhaps wished they could have turned back. In interviewing others about migration experiences, women can identify what sustained them through this, and they can develop knowledges about what circumstances are most favourable to perseverance. Further, they can get a keener sense of how far down the track they might be before feeling that they are breaking from some of the insecurity, confusion and disorientation that is associated with these migrations.

Planning a celebration at the point of arrival at the journey's end can also assist in establishing these circumstances. This planning can extend all the way through to putting together the invitation list, and even to preparing the invitations.

Chris: You have talked about the difficulties that survivors of abuse often have in developing supportive networks, and the negative meanings they often give to their need for help. Could you say something about this?

Michael: Many of the women I meet, and the men as well, who have been subject to abuse historically, are rather critical of themselves for what they see as their "dependent natures". They tend to pathologise themselves through various self-accusations for what they construe to be their dependency on others. At times, this is the concern that has been the basis for seeking the consultation. "Dependency" is a problem that is presented to be "resolved", and, in resolving this, people expect to reach a destination in their life at which they can "stand on their own two feet".

Now I often find this definition of the problem and this conclu-sion about the solution to be somewhat curious. Could it be that these definitions and these conclusions are informed by and reached through dominant cultural notions of what it means to be a real person - that is, "independent", "self-possessed", "self-contained", "self-actualising" etc. - and dominant cultural notions of how this might be achieved - that is, through separation?

My response to such self-accusations is often to take notes about "abuse team" membership over the course of the person's life, and notes about the operations of, and the period of operations of, this abuse team. This makes it possible for me to calculate the "weightiness" of the abuse team and its work through simple multiplication - that is, the number of abuse team members operative by the level of their operations by the period of these operations. Membership includes all of those who were centrally and peripherally involved, including those who were complicit with the abuse, if not active in its perpetration. Then, together we can determine what might provide a counterweight to the abuse team. Now, it is logical that the establishment of a "nurturing team" could provide such a counterweight, and eventually tip the balance in the person's favour. It becomes possible to determine, through calculation, the requirements for nurturing team activity and membership. Certain projections can be made about these requirements through a calculation in which duration of involvement of, intensity of activity of, and the number of, nurturing team members are all linked in an inverse relationship - so it makes sense to include more people in the nurturing team, rather than less.

So, in this work, what people have determined to be dependency is reinterpreted. People step into alternative discourses about identity. Whatever "dependency" was, it is no longer some psychological fact of the person's life that needs to be "worked through", and the practices of self-accusation associated with this recede. It becomes possible for people to approach those whom they have believed they were dependent upon, and to formally extend an invitation to them to join the nurturing team. As well, nurturing team membership can be increased by encouraging people to identify and to approach others whom they think might be willing to join. If, after these steps there is a shortfall in membership, therapists can put people in touch with others who are "card carrying" nurturing team members who would be willing to play a part.

When prospective members receive formal invitations to join such teams, they are less likely to experience being burdened, and it is more likely that they will look forward to the first nurturing team meeting so that they can discuss their contribution. Upon receipt of this invitation, they are also far more likely to experience acknowledgement for their contribution to date. And it helps if, in the formal invitations, the nurturing work that they have already contributed is acknowledged.

Chris: So, what do these nurturing team meetings look like?

Michael: First, the person who has issued the invitations provides some account of the abuse team's membership, its activities, the duration of these activities, and the long-term effects of these activities. Second, the notion of the nurturing team is introduced, along with some thoughts about the part that this team could have to play in undoing the work of the abuse team. Third, the work that has already been done in this direction by prospective nurturing team members is acknowledged, along with the effects of this work. Fourth, prospective team members then talk about the sort of ongoing contribution to nurturing work that they believe might challenge the work of the abuse team, and that might fit with the necessities of their own lives in a way that would not be burdensome to them. Fifth, the person who called the meeting responds to these proposals, and makes further suggestions about what might work best for them. Sixth, all of these proposals and suggestions are negotiated, and plans are made for their introduction. At this time, these plans are worked through in their particularities.

Chris: Do you join these meetings?

Michael: I think that it is very important for the therapist to be present for at least the first of these meetings, to provide support and clarification. For therapists, as much as for the team members and for the person who called the meeting, these occasions can be deeply moving.

Chris: I suppose that this process of formalisation has a considerable effect on the morale of the team.

Michael: Yes. The team members experience stepping into more of a proactive role, one that doesn't exhaust - for example, one team member might enjoy expressing their artistic skills in making cards with messages that counter the "voices" of the abuse team, cards that the person who convened the nurturing team can receive in the mail three times a week. This proactive role is one in which the nurturing team member's central contribution is no longer one of responding to crises. Besides, the person who has convened the nurturing team experiences fewer crises once the work of these teams is under way.

Chris: Do you think that the development of nurturing teams is particularly important in the period of time when a survivor of abuse is engaged in the migration of identity you spoke about earlier?

Michael: Yes, I think it is particularly important. It contributes to conditions that are favourable to perseverance and to hope, to conditions under which people are less likely to see themselves as a drain on others, and under which they are more able to just reach out and to take advantage of the support that is available.

Chris: I'd like to change the subject and ask a few questions about how you see the therapeutic relationship. I know you think it's important that the built-in power differences between the therapist and the client be openly recognised and addressed. Could you say why you see this as important, and how you approach this?

Michael: There's always a power differential within the therapeutic context, regardless of how committed we are to dismantling this, regardless of how determined we might be to establish this context as an egalitarian one. The acknowledgement of this brings to therapists a realisation that it is up to them to do their best to find ways of ensuring that this power differential doesn't have untoward effects on the lives of the people who consult them.

I am often consulted by men and women who have survived abuse, and there's great potential for this inherent power differential to have negative effects on these people's lives, and to reproduce some of the experiences that have been so subjugating of them. So, it is imperative that I talk with people about the possible negative effects of this power differential in the therapeutic context, and about how we might build in structures to mitigate these possibilities. But as well, and this perhaps is a more primary consideration, there is the fact that I'm a man and it's usually men who perpetrate the abuses that we have been talking of in this interview. So, I also need to talk to those who consult me about how this fact might introduce certain hazards to the therapeutic interaction, about how this fact could possibly lead to the inadvertent reproduction of past experiences of domination and of disqualification.

Chris: What do you talk about that draws attention to the potential hazards in this work that are the outcome of your gender?

Michael: This depends entirely upon the circumstances at hand, and can be informed by a developing appreciation of the person's experience of the politics of gender. In response to this I might find myself talking about my understanding of the extent to which the behaviour of others is so often governed by the mood of "senior" men - or, if you like, by a senior man's display of mood - and of the extent to which there are possibilities that some of my responses might be read as mood-related, and might be experienced as somehow controlling of the person, or disqualifying of the their knowledgeableness in the context of therapy. Or, in other circumstances, I might find myself speculating about entirely different hazards. In reviewing potential hazards such as these, plans can be worked out for monitoring them, drawing attention to them should they be recognised by either party, and for addressing them within the context of therapy.

But, this sort of acknowledgement of these possible dangers and limitations of this work is not enough. I believe that we need be thorough in our efforts to build in practices and structures of accountability. I have described some of these practices and structures of accountability in a piece entitled *A conversation about accountability*, and will not review them here.

Chris: Just picking up on what you have been saying about the mood of the "senior male", I think that it is particularly important for us to recognise the extent to which interactions in families may be governed by the mood of the father, and the extent to which this can play itself out in therapeutic contexts when families are consulting therapists. I've heard you make similar observations. And I think I've heard you talking about the importance of therapists recognising the extent to which their participation might be governed by these moods. Have I heard you correctly on this?

Michael: That's correct. When working with families, or for that matter, when working with heterosexual couples, I believe that it is important for therapists to be aware of this issue. We all have experiences of the dominant men's culture, and many aspects of this experience are profoundly negative. My guess is that most of the readers of this transcript could readily relate stories about circumstances of their lives under which what they've said and how they have acted has been considerably determined by the moods of some senior male. And a very great number of us have been taught to fear and to be beware of these moods. So, when confronted by the moods of senior men, we are somewhat vulnerable to stepping into behaviour that goes against our own better judgement, that compromises our chosen values, that violates our relationships with our "selves".

So, it makes a great deal of sense for us to take responsibility for the monitoring of our responses to the senior men in therapeutic contexts. This affords some chance of determining whether or not our perceptions of the man's mood are determining of our responses in this work. Needless to say, if these moods are determining of our responses to the other members of the families that consult us, then we are undoubtedly contributing to their experience of oppression.

Chris: As part of the increasingly widespread claims that men's experience is being ignored in the process of paying attention to women's experience, I've heard it stated recently by both men and some women that mothers are just as likely as fathers, or even more likely, to abuse young children. Could you comment on your experience in this area, and how you see the context of these claims?

Michael: I think that these claims are very much part of a general backlash. These claims are achieved by blurring certain important distinctions around the definition of abuse. Many researchers seem committed to blurring this distinction. For many years, I have worked with women and men who have been abused, and who have experienced this abuse under a range of circumstances. And almost invariably the abuse has been perpetrated by men.

Now, I know that it has been said that women and men find it more difficult to reveal abuse by their mothers than by their fathers, but this doesn't make a great deal of sense. I've not heard one convincing reason for men and women to have more difficulty in revealing abuse by their mothers than by their fathers. In fact, because in our culture it has generally been expected that the fathers are the disciplinarians, and that they may legitimately resort to corporal methods, I believe that women's attempts at the disciplining of children are more likely to be read as abuse than are men's. In fact, it seems only rarely that the abuses that men perpetrate in the name of discipline get read as abuse.

Add to this consideration the fact that this culture of ours is a "mother-blaming culture" - I do not believe that it is possible to successfully refute this fact. Under this circumstance, I have not a doubt that any abuses that are perpetrated by mothers are far more likely to be taken up and placed under the microscope than are the abuses that are perpetrated by fathers. So, I think that this claim that you are referring to is a spurious claim, and, as I have said, part of a general, and at times well-organised, backlash against the voices of women on the issue of abuse.

Chris: So, what would you say about the experiences of those men who have in actual fact been seriously abused by a female person in their lives? Because what you've just said could possibly read as a disqualification of their experience.

Michael: I do hope that nothing that I have said at any point in this interview is experienced as disqualification of men's experiences when they have been abused by women, or of women's experiences when they have been abused by women. I have worked with men and with women who have experienced abuse from their mothers, and other women, and, in this circumstance, have attended as carefully to the articulation of this as I have to the articulation of any other experiences of abuse.

Chris: There are more questions that I would like to ask, about other aspects of your work with people who have survived abuse. Is that okay?

Michael: I have appreciated your questions so far, and they have provided me with the opportunity to articulate many of my thoughts about this work. But right now I need a break. Perhaps we could get back to some of these other questions on another occasion. Could I also suggest that you might be interested in reading Sheridan Linnell and Dorothy Cora's *Discoveries: A group resource guide for women who have been sexually abused in childhood*. This resource guide is a good source of information about practical and creative applications of this work within the narrative tradition.

Chris: Okay, I'll look for this. And let's make some plans to meet again about this work. Thank you, Michael.

REFERENCE

Linnell, S. & Cora, D. 1993:
  Discoveries: A group resource guide for women who have been sexually abused in childhood. Sydney: Dympna House Publications.

5.   Psychotic Experience and Discourse*
Interviewer: Ken Stewart * *

Ken: In the interview of 1990 I asked about your theory of pathology. You responded to this question with:

> *The word makes me wince! When I hear it, I think about the spectacular success of clinical medicine in the objectification of persons and of their bodies, and the extent to which the pathologising of persons is the most common and taken-for-granted practice in the mental health/welfare disciplines, and the central and most major achievement of the psychologies.*

Would your response be similar today?

Michael: I wouldn't take back what I said in that interview of a few years ago. There now exists a simply fantastic number of opportunities that are available to mental health professionals for the pathologising of people's lives. Due to an extraordinary investment in the development of the dis-

---

*   This is, in a sense, an interview within an interview. Some of the questions asked here are based on an earlier interview that was conducted in 1990, but was never completed.

**   Ken Stewart is from the Family Treatment Program at Human Services, Inc, Washington County, Minnesota, and is adjunct faculty at the Minnesota School for Professional Psychology.

---

courses of pathology, we now have at our disposal a vast array of ways of speaking with and interacting with people that reproduce the subject/object dualism that is so pervasive in the structuring of relations in our culture.

These ways of speaking and interacting with people puts them on the other side of knowledge, on the outside. These ways of speaking and acting make it possible for mental health professionals to construct people as the objects of psychiatric knowledge, to contribute to a sense of identity which has "otherness" as its central feature. The success of these discourses is beyond question, and I believe that this achievement represents one of the truly great marginalisations of contemporary culture.

Ken: In our field, we are currently seeing a great deal of interest in post-modern thought. Do you think these postmodern influences are having much of an impact on various pathologising discourses?

Michael: As you say, there have been significant developments of this sort. However, I'm not at all sure that these have yet gone very far in challenging the hegemony of the pathologising discourses, which are undergoing constant processes of revision, refinement and elaboration.

Ken: Where does this leave us? Is there a way to address traditional conceptions of the so-called mental illnesses such as schizophrenia, obsessive-compulsive disorder, the histrionic personality disorder, and other personality disorders from the Axis II personality disorders of the DSM-IV, without pathologising people? Do those of us who embrace the social constructionist perspective have to leave this domain to the authors of the psychiatric knowledges, or do we make some kind of counter-claim to this territory? And, if we do, how do we address the phenomena that these classifications refer to? Do you think that family therapy has something to offer here?

Michael: Perhaps I could take your last question first. For some reason, in the critique of the institutions that have played a key role in the maintenance and in the reproduction of these pathologising discourses, family therapy exempts itself. It has so often considered itself on the outside of these discourses of pathology. But I do not believe that family therapy's claim to this exempt status can be sustained.

Historically, family therapy has embraced formal systems of analysis that are informed by the metaphors of "system", "dynamics", "structure", and so on. These metaphors provide for an "expert" interpretation of the events and of the experiences of people's lives, and have been deployed to invoke notions of family or relational "disorder", "dysfunction", and "pathology". And these metaphors have encouraged us to position ourselves in relation to others in a way that also reproduces the subject/object dualism that I have already referred to.

Ken: There have been many critiques of these and other pathologising discourses - both from within and outside the field. Yet, despite this, they continue to dominate all other discourses that have tried to offer alternatives. How do you understand this?

Michael: Yes, there have been many critiques. Perhaps it would be useful here to review one or two of these.

First, there is the issue of the self-presentation of the mental health professional. It has been said that to demonstrate a degree of "mastery" in the ways of speaking about other people's lives that are informed by these pathologising discourses, and to demonstrate a degree of skill in those ways of acting towards others that are informed by these discourses, accords these professionals a small grant of moral worth in their own communities. The achievement of this mastery, and the demonstration of this skill, brings with it the experience of esteem in the eyes of one's colleagues.

Second, it has been argued that to demonstrate this mastery and these skills opens the door to a world of career opportunities, and to economic opportunities. So, the demonstration of "diagnostic acumen" turns out to be highly rewarding - it is lucrative and it provides access to institutional power. But, more than this, here in North America it has become a necessity. It is now becoming virtually impossible for mental health professionals to earn a living if they don't subject their work to the DSM III-R, or whatever the latest version of this is.

Third, it can be argued that, since the pathologising discourses are cloaked in an impressive language that establishes claims to an objective reality, these discourses make it possible for mental health professionals to avoid facing the real effects of, or the consequences of, these ways of speaking about and acting towards those people who consult them. If our work has to do with the idea of subjecting persons to "truth", then this renders invisible to us the consequences of how we speak to people about their lives, and of how we structure our interactions with them; this mantle of "truth" makes it possible for us to avoid reflecting on the implications of our constructions and of our therapeutic interactions in regard to the shaping of people's lives. In this way, pathologising discourses make it possible for mental health professionals to avoid accountability, and to retain and to extend on their monopoly on power.

These are but a few of the many possible critiques. But, aside from these, there are other considerations that may account for the extraordinary development of, and success of, these pathologising discourses. Pathologising discourses have the potential to bring to us a degree of comfort in a world in which it is becoming increasingly difficult to find this. These discourses make it possible to define those problems for which people seek help as aberrations. As such, they assist us to avoid the acknowledgement of the fact that these problems are very significantly of our culture, that these problems are products of our modes of life and of thought. The discourses of pathology make it possible for us to ignore the extent to which the problems for which people seek therapy are the outcome of certain practices of relationship and practices of the self, many of which are actually informed by modern notions of "individualism". And the discourses of pathology make it possible for us to ignore the extent to which the problems for which people seek help are so often mired in the structures of inequality of our culture, including those pertaining to gender, race, ethnicity, class, economics, age, and so on.

If we can see the difficulties for which people seek help as the outcome of some aberration rather than a product of our ways of thought and ways of life, we can avoid facing our complicity in the maintenance of these ways of life and of thought. This assists us to disavow our complicity in the constitution of the worlds we share with others. In obscuring this link between the problems for which people seek help and the modes of life and thought of our culture, we can avoid facing the responsibility that we have to take action to address the context of people's lives, and we can avoid facing the responsibility that we have to dismantle the various structures of inequality that are associated with these.

Ken: Okay. So, let's get down to some of the specifics of your work. I've heard it said that you are opposed to the use of labels and to the use of medications.

Michael: Now that's interesting. I've heard the very same opinion about my position on these matters.

Ken: Well?

Michael: From time to time I hear things about what I have said that I haven't spoken of, and from time to time I read accounts of my thought that do not relate to what I think. And at times I hear accounts of my conduct that are not at all close to my experience of it.

Ken: What's an example of this last point?

Michael: Several years ago, there was a story going around that, during a consultation in Canada, I had externalized a problem with a person who had a diagnosis of paranoid schizophrenia, and that, in response to this, I had been beaten up. What actually did happen was that I had intervened in an assault, in order to prevent the perpetration of grievous bodily harm, and had my face split open in the process. Furthermore, none of this had anything to do with a consultation.

Ken: Sounds simply awful! So tell me, what is your position on labels and medication?

Michael: In regard to drugs, I have not taken a general position on the so-called anti psychotic medications. Instead, I have been far more interested to find what is enabling for people in regard to this question - and here I am using the word "enabling" in its positive sense. This consideration leads to specific questions:

- *How might one go about assisting people to determine whether these drugs are contributing to their quality of life, or whether they are subtracting from this?*
- *How might one go about assisting people to determine in which ways these drugs might be enabling, and in which ways they might be disabling?*
- *How might one go about assisting people to monitor the effects of different medications, and of different levels of these medications?*
- *How might one go about assisting people to evaluate the real effects of these medications on their lives and in their relationships with others?*
- *How might one go about assisting people to establish what might be for them suitable criteria for such an evaluation?*
- *How might one go about assisting people to fully inform themselves about the various negative side-effects of these drugs?*
- *How might one go about assisting people to identify which people are most invested in compliance with regimes of medications, which people are least invested in this, and the particular interests of these parties?*

These are just a sample of the many, many questions that can be appropriately asked about drugs.

I do hope that this discussion goes some way towards challenging the view that I am opposed to the use of drugs. I have witnessed drugs being used in ways that have a profound effect in opening up the horizons of people's lives, in ways that bring a range of new possibilities for action. And I have also witnessed drugs being used in ways that are primarily for the purposes of social control, in ways that subtract very significantly from people's possibilities for action, in ways that dispossess people of choice.

Ken: And what are your thoughts on various labels used in the field of mental health?

Michael: If you are talking about making psychiatric diagnoses, I have no interest whatsoever in trafficking in this trade. In regard to labels in general, and people's use of them, questions similar to those we have just been talking about with regard to drugs seem appropriate.

In responding to questions of this sort, I am mindful of the fact that some people do find such labels enabling. This has been interpreted in a variety of ways. For example, it is said that illness labels undermine the various self-accusations and attributions of personal inadequacy that are experienced by people who are not able to live out their lives in the customary ways. Furthermore, it is said that these labels make it possible for persons to break from the stress of the expectations that they would be subject to if they were "well". And it is frequently argued that psychiatric diagnoses serve to dissolve the guilt that is so often experienced by relatives, and that this has the effect of undermining self-defeating behaviours and of promoting more constructive interactions in familial contexts.

And, while I can appreciate these arguments, and have no difficulty in honouring what people have to say about some of the positive effects of psychiatric diagnoses, I have no doubt that these outcomes provide for some interesting reflection on our culture - that, in order for people to break from these self-accusations and attributions of personal inadequacy, from the stress that is informed by the expectations about what it means to be a real person in our culture, and from the experiences of guilt that we have discussed, they must step into the site of "illness". Illness is a site of culture, one that is structured, one that brings with it particular modes of life and of thought. It is a site of culture that shapes life.

So, diagnosis provides for an exemption that is permissible through illness. But this is a sad reflection on our culture, and I do think that we can do a lot to assist people to find other alternative sites in this culture in which they can succeed in breaking from dominant ways of being and thinking, alternative sites that bring with them other options for how they might lead their lives, options that do not require exemption through illness.

And it is very interesting that, in the work that we do together to identify these other sites, sites that are often defined through the tracing of histories of resistance to dominant culture, the diagnosis itself becomes increasingly irrelevant, and the exemption it brings with it becomes increasingly unnecessary for living.

Ken: So, what happens when you are consulted by people who seem to identify with their psychiatric diagnosis?

Michael: I do not want to be misunderstood on this point. If I am consulting with a person who prefers to use such labels, then I am interested in honouring what they experience this to be doing for them, and I am interested in actively exploring with them what speaking about themselves in this way makes possible.

Ken: But, since these labels co-operate in the colonising of people's lives - treating them as an "other" that is at once "knowable and visible" - I would have assumed that you would be opposed to them altogether.

Michael: Well, it is difficult to be in opposition to labels *per se*. In language, there is always naming, and so we always have labels of one sort or another. What is of critical importance, however, is the nature of the discourses that are associated with this naming. A consideration of discourse takes us to specific questions about any naming. What knowledges are privileged in a particular process of naming, and what knowledges are rendered irrelevant or are disqualified in this process? Who is qualified to speak and to name, and under what circumstances is it acceptable for them to do so? What relational practices and techniques of power are associated with acts of naming, of diagnosing, and what are the real effects, on people's lives, of these practices and techniques? And so on. Here I have been trying to emphasise the extent to which it is discourse that is of vital consideration.

Of course, the labels associated with one discourse can be usurped by taking them up into alternative discourses. This is often achieved by marginalised groups. When these labels are taken up and inserted into an alternative discourse, they often become terms of pride, and ones that represent certain lifestyle choices and knowledges about ways of being and thinking. This has the effect of taking such labels a long way from the mainstream discourse that had been so subjugating of people in marginalised groups.

Ken: So then, in my mind at least, these thoughts take me to considerations of aetiology. What is your position on aetiology?

Michael: In seventeen of the last twenty or so years I have had formal relations with mainstream psychiatric services - I have worked in state psychiatric hospitals and in child and adolescent psychiatric services, and have spent a considerable period of time consulting to a large state psychiatric hospital. And, in addition to this, at Dulwich Centre we have a small independent community mental health project. Now, let me tell you something that you might find surprising. Throughout this entire period, in the totality of my experience of these different psychiatric contexts, the only times that I have witnessed considerations of aetiology having any effect on management whatsoever have been on those relatively few occasions upon which a brain lesion of some sort has been suspected. Even medication is a trial-and-error affair. I say that you might find this surprising, because, despite the general irrelevance of considerations of aetiology, anyone who has worked for mainstream psychiatric services will have witnessed an extraordinary amount of time and energy devoted to these considerations.

So, what are we to conclude about this? Perhaps such considerations of aetiology are a hallmark of the performance of psychiatric knowledge because these considerations provide opportunities for the scientising of this knowledge.

Ken: So, you don't have a position on aetiology?

Michael: To answer your question, I have always resisted taking a position on the aetiology of the so-called psychiatric disorders. In fact, I have consistently refused the incitement that I have experienced to step into a position on this, and to enter into debates and other activities that depend upon such positions. I am willing to consider most notions of aetiology, but, quite frankly, these considerations are as irrelevant to what I do in this work as they are for others.

Ken: Does this mean that you are even willing to entertain some of the current biological notions of aetiology for what is referred to as schizophrenia?

Michael: Of course! Of course! But this is not relevant to what I do.

Ken: So, what do you do? In taking the position that you do on psychiatric discourses, isn't there a risk that you wind up excluding yourself from participation in this field? Isn't it possible that, in this way, you will cancel out your own contribution? Doesn't this leave you with nothing to say?

Michael: Certainly not. I am simply talking about standing outside of the territory as it is defined by psychiatric knowledge, and as it is structured by pathologising discourses. I am not talking about standing apart from people and their experiences, including those experiences that are so often taken up into pathologising discourses.

Ken: Okay, what are our options?

Michael: I think that we can assist people to challenge the hegemony of the psychiatric knowledges. We can work with them to identify the extent that their own lives are "knowledged". We can engage people in conversations that are honouring of their knowledges of life, and that trace the history of their knowledgeableness. We can join people in conversations that provide the opportunity for them to build on these knowledges, and that assist people to develop plans for applying this knowledgeableness to those experiences that they find troubling.

We can make it our business to work collaboratively with people in identifying those ways of speaking about their lives that contribute to a sense of personal agency, and that contribute to the experience of being an authority on one's life. And we can assist people to draw distinctions around these ways of speaking and those other ways of speaking that contribute to experiences of marginalisation, that subtract from a sense of personal agency, and that undermine an appreciation of one's authoritativeness.

Rather than referencing what we do to the sort of formal systems of analysis that we have already discussed, we can strive to build on those developments in our work that are more referenced to people's experiences of life, including of psychotic phenomena. We can find ways of attending more directly to people's experiences of life.

And we can join with people in challenging those relations of power that inform the subject/object dualism that I referred to earlier in this conversation.

Ken: Take this last point. Say something more about how this might be achieved.

Michael: I'll float one example here, one that relates to the idea of returning the "gaze", or turning the gaze back on itself. For those people who are the recipients of ward rounds, for them to research these ward rounds can be very empowering. This might engage them in a study of who can speak, under what circumstances they can speak, which ways of speaking are acknowledged, which ways of speaking are disqualified, whose authority is privileged, the effects of the privileging of this voice, and so on. I find that many people are quite taken by the introduction of this idea, and that it has a positive effect even if it is not taken up in any formalised way. It appears that even to think the unthinkable goes some way towards undoing the effects of the marginalisation to which people have been subject. Of course, there are many other ways in which the gaze can be returned.

Ken: This is a subversive idea if I ever heard one.

Michael: Yes, this might be quite subversive. But practices of returning the gaze do not have to be covert, and they are not necessarily antagonistic to the efforts of the staff of psychiatric institutions. In fact, these practices can serve mental health professionals well in their efforts to establish contexts that are healing. In that these practices of returning the gaze can have the effect of rendering transparent many of the otherwise taken-for-granted ideas and practices of psychiatric contexts, they can be of great assistance to staff who experience a commitment to confront the moral and ethical responsibility for the real effects of their interactions on the lives of those people who are seeking help. When mental health professionals accept the fact that they can never be certain that they are not reproducing, in their work, the circumstances that provide the context of the very problems for which people are seeking help, they will experience a degree of relief in the feedback and the possibilities for action that are afforded by these practices of returning the gaze.

Ken: You also mentioned possibilities for being more experience-based in working with people who have defined psychiatric conditions. So, could you give me an example of what this experience-based work might look like with schizophrenia? And could you also say what distinguishes this from accepted approaches to this phenomenon?

Michael: In regard to the generally accepted approaches, I have noted a strong bias in regard to the psychotic experience itself. This is an anti-experience bias. I believe that the idea of talking to people about their psychotic experiences has had rather bad press over the past few decades. Within this context, it is not surprising that some of the proposals that I have put forward on talking to people about their subjective experience of psychotic episodes have provoked disquiet.

Ken: Maybe some fear that you would be reifying the delusions instead of talking people out of them. How has this sort of response impacted on your work?

Michael: It hasn't really. Some have expressed their apprehension about my practices of relating to psychotic experience, and, at times, have been somewhat perturbed by my unwillingness to desist in my further exploration of ways of talking to people about their experience of psychotic episodes. However, I have never found the content of such responses to be at all persuasive.

Ken: In some of your workshops, you have referred to the work that you do in assisting people to revise their relationship with their auditory hallucinations, or their "voices". Is this one of the developments that has come from this exploration of psychotic experiences?

Michael: Yes it is. Assisting people to revise their relationship with their voices is usually a very significant part of the interactions that I have with people who have the diagnosis of schizophrenia. The successful revision of this relationship invariably has a powerful effect on the quality of these people's lives, and, in my experience, it generally plays a considerable role in reducing their vulnerability to relapse as well.

Ken: If this is so, is this a practice that is being taken up more by mental health professionals?

Michael: Yes. I have contact with many mental health professionals who have been taking these ideas up in unique contexts and in unique ways. As an example of how this is being done in working with groups of people who have psychiatric diagnoses and who are considered to be "chronically ill", I would refer you to the *Worthy of Discussion* groups of Gaye Stockell and Marilyn O'Neil from Sydney, and to the developments that they and their colleagues have been putting together in establishing more collaborative approaches in the rehabilitation context.

And I have contact with others who are enthusiastically exploring the fit between some of these ideas and practices, their own original contributions, and some of the more established ideas and practices in this field. For an example of such work I would refer you to Chris Beels and Margaret Newmark of New York, and to David Moltz of Portland, Maine.

As well, I know some administrators, managers, and clinical directors who have been effective in changing the face of the broader provision of psychiatric services by incorporating the sort of ideas and practices referred to here with a number of other related ideas and practices. A good person for you to talk to, who has achieved a great deal in this area, is Alan Rosen of Sydney.

But there are many other initiatives apart from these. One quite recent initiative is the work that Stephen Madigan, David Epston and the Anti-Anorexia League have been doing together in British Columbia - work that is having what I understand to be a transformative effect on policy with regard to the treatment of anorexia nervosa and bulimia.

Ken: These developments all sound exciting, and I would like to learn more about them. So I take it you haven't been too discouraged in your work in this area?

Michael: Definitely not. Over the years, I have experienced a good measure of support and encouragement from many people, and this has been sustaining.

However, I will say that my efforts to share more generally, with others, what people have had to say about this work have yielded mixed responses. So, at times, I haven't found things all that straightforward.

Ken: Give me an example of what you mean.

Michael: Well, in regard to the work that I have been developing on the revision of people's relationship with their voices, for some years, in certain circles, I did experience constraints in presenting my findings. These constraints were partly born of scepticism and of doubt, and were partly political in nature.

However, several years ago, articles began to be published in mainstream journals that called attention to the need to consider the subjective experience of those persons who received a diagnosis of schizophrenia, and that also called attention to the significance of the quality of the person's relationship with their voices. In fact, one journal devoted an entire issue to these explorations (see the *Schizophrenia Bulletin*, Volume 15, Number 2, 1989). While these articles did not describe processes that contributed to possibilities for people to revise their relationship with their voices, some of the findings were supportive of what I was doing, and, since the publication of articles like these, I have found it somewhat easier to talk about this work in psychiatric contexts.

Ken: So how do you explain this - that having a different relationship with one's voices can make a significant difference in terms of the severity of the psychotic episode?

Michael: In part, I believe that it relates to culture. Although it seems relatively easy for us to entertain the idea that much of what we think and believe, and much of what we do, is informed by culture, for some reason it seems rather more difficult for us to entertain the idea that psychotic phenomena are similarly informed; that, regardless of aetiology, the content, form and expression of psychotic phenomena, such as auditory hallucinations, are shaped by culture. When it becomes less difficult to entertain this idea, it becomes possible for us to appreciate the extent to which culture is just as shaping of the lives of people who have whatever it is that schizophrenia is.

Ken: Give me an example of this.

Michael: There is nothing about physiology or genetics that would pre-dispose the voices of schizophrenia to attack their female subjects on the basis of their sexuality, or to call their male subjects "wimps". And there is nothing about physiology that would predispose the voices of schizophrenia to see others as adversaries, and their subjects as possessions. Those auditory hallucinations that people find most troublesome are so often distinctly patriarchal in their attitudes and their techniques of power. This is so for the voices that harass men and those that harass women. These voices are overwhelmingly evaluative of people; they are critical and disqualifying; they rate highly on expectations of people and low on acknowledgement.

Ken: You state that these voices are distinctly patriarchal. Could you say more about how they speak?

Michael: Okay, but I would like to emphasise the fact that I am not referring to all of the voices of schizophrenia here. In this work, it is essential to assist people to distinguish those voices that are controlling and dominating from those voices that are supportive, or that at least have the potential to be supportive.

Ken: Alright, but I would like to come back to this distinction later.

Michael: Those voices that are troublesome are highly opinionated and quite convincing. They rely on certain devices in order to speak impressively, in order to secure unquestionable authority, in order to establish claims to objective knowledge, in order to convince their subject that they alone can grasp the truth of people's natures, desires, purposes, and so on.

Ken: Can you say more about these devices? They sound scary.

Michael: The impressive ways of speaking to which I am referring are "at large", and we could refer to them as the "disembodied" ways of speaking. I am sure that these will be familiar to the readers of the transcript of this interview. These ways of speaking have been called disembodied because they disclaim any reference to context, because they allow one to establish knowledge claims that are considered to be context-independent. They have the effect of elevating specific knowledge claims to a certainty or "truth" status, and of disqualifying those knowledges that are represented in more situated ways of speaking.

Ken: Ah, yes - those who claim to speak the "truth" about all situations, regardless of context, an all-too-familiar experience that many of us have been subjected to. Still, I think that recent developments in the field have attempted to expose these "temptations of certainty". Could you say more about this kind of a-contextual way of speaking.

Michael: The devices that are associated with these "expert" ways of speaking include those that (a) obscure the motives or purposes that are associated with one's speech acts, (b) delete all reference to the personal experiences through which one's knowledge claims are generated, (c) exclude information about the personal and interpersonal struggles and dilemmas that are associated with the construction of one's preferred realities (this includes the erasure of the personal experiences of contestation and argumentation through which one's knowledge claims are established), (d) divert attention from the personal investments that are informed by one's location in the social worlds of gender, race, culture, class, work, sexual preference, and so on, and (e) delete all reference to the history of controversy and dissent that surrounds all "global" knowledge claims.

Ken: And what are the implications of this in this work?

Michael: Well, disembodied speech acts can be very disempowering of those who are subject to them. They are quite capturing. They severely limit and constrict possible responses. However, the persuasiveness and impressiveness of such speech acts can be undermined by the principle of embodiment; that is, by situating these speech acts within the context of the speaker's (a) motives and purposes, (b) personal experiences, including those that relate to dilemmas and other struggles that the speaker has experienced in the process of attributing meaning to their experiences of life, (c) investments that are informed by their location in the social worlds of gender, culture, race, class, sexual preference, and so on, and also by bringing forth the history of controversy that surrounds the speaker's objective knowledge claims.

Ken: Knowing your work as I do, I'll bet that you have some interesting questions that would uncover and deconstruct some of these truth claims.

Michael: Yes. We can ask questions that insist on embodiment, questions that require speakers to situate their opinions.

Ken: Could you give some examples of these questions?

Michael: Okay. To encourage speakers to situate their opinions in the context of their purposes, we could ask questions like: *So you have a strong opinion about what I should do. Tell me, in voicing your opinion in this way, what effect do you hope this might have on what I do?* Or maybe we could ask: *If you were to succeed in influencing what I do on this occasion, how would this fit with your overall goals for my life?* Or perhaps: *I think that I have some understanding of how you would like your opinion to shape what I do right now. How does this fit with your general purposes for my life? How does this fit with your plans for my life?*

To encourage speakers to situate their opinions in the context of their lived experience, we could try something like: *Could you tell me about some of your personal experiences of life that have played a central role in the formation of this opinion? This would be helpful to me, as I would then know more about how to take your opinion, and I might be able to identify those parts of your views that could fit for me. Perhaps I could then talk of some of my own experiences of life, and share with you some of the conclusions that I have reached from all of this.*

To encourage speakers to situate their opinions within the context of their location in the social world, we might try something like: *In which circles are these sort of opinions most strongly held? Do all of the people in these circles agree with this opinion? If some of these people were here with us, how would they go about supporting your opinion? What do you think would happen if, in their presence, you were to dissent? What sort of pressure do you think you would experience to conform, to recant? What consequences do you think you would be facing if you didn't agree to do so?*

But this is just a small sample of the possibilities for ways of responding that are deconstructing of the "truths" that are championed in disembodied speech acts. And I want to emphasise that these questions do not require an answer in order to be effective. In asking such questions, those who are subject to disembodied speech acts become less captive, and are confronted with new possibilities for action.

Ken: Those are great questions! I have some ideas about how I can put some to use right away. Members of my team often come across persons in social service or medical circles for whom these questions would be very appropriate. Can you tie these ideas back to the question of working with people who experience auditory hallucinations?

Michael: As I have already mentioned, when these voices are most troublesome, they speak impressively and persuasively. At the times that these voices are most troublesome, they succeed in convincing their subjects that they speak with authority, with objective knowledge; that they speak of the truth of life and of the world, of the truth of their subject's identity, of the truth of the motives of others, and so on. These impressive voices so often succeed in capturing their subject, and in disqualifying their subject's special knowledges of life. And this is usually traumatising and disempowering of everyone concerned.

In these circumstances it makes sense to de-authorise these impressive voices, to disempower them, and this can be achieved through the embodiment of their "truths". We can encourage the people who are the subjects of these voices to insist that the voices embody their demands, requirements, opinions, investments, and so on. Such embodiment can be achieved by assisting those who are in the subject position to situate these voices within the context of the voices' purposes, their experiences, and their history.

Ken: You speak of these voices as if they are independent entities.

Michael: Yes. In fact, in this work, the deconstruction of the "truths" of these voices can be achieved best through the personification of them. Or perhaps I should say that this is achieved through the extension of this personification, as it is not at all unusual for those people who are the subjects of these voices to have personified them in advance of our meeting - except that the purposes of these voices have not, until this time, been at all transparent.

Ken: Many people understand your work primarily involving various aspects of externalizing conversations with people - in which the problem is not only externalized, but personified in unique ways. This fits with other theorists and clinicians who speak of internalized voices and "objects" or representations of significant persons and relationships in our lives. So you externalize the hidden, more pernicious, aspects of what previously had been internalized or introjected. Is this way of personifying the problem a regular part of your practice?

Michael: Let me answer your question this way. This practice of personification is but one way of re-voicing the problem, and, for me, this re-voicing of the problem is an important aspect of the work that I do. I know that if we engage with people in the re-voicing of the problems that they consult us about, this provides them, and us as well, with the opportunity to establish an appreciation of the politics of the person's experience of life.

Ken: So, how do you proceed, in practice, with this re-voicing of the problem?

Michael: Mostly via the formulation of questions like:

* *What is it that the voices are trying to convince you of at this time? What are they trying to talk you into? How does this fit with their overall*

plans for your life?

- *How do the voices expect their assertions, their "shoulds", to affect what you do? If they succeed in forcing their will on your life, how do you imagine this might influence the direction of your life?*
- *Are these voices for you having your own opinion, knowing what you want, or are they against you having your own opinion?*
- *I do appreciate that these voices throw you into confusion. In whose service is this confusion? Does it contribute to their goals for your life, or does this favour or clarify your own goals?*

As you can see, through questions like this, distinctions can be drawn around different desires, purposes, intentions, goals, and so on. These distinctions make it more possible for people to determine the extent to which these fit with the designs of the dominant voices, and the extent to which they fit with the sort of designs that are preferred by the person concerned. Even confusion is found to be in the service of these voices, rather than in the service of the person. In drawing such distinctions, persons achieve some degree of clarity about a preferred account of what they want for their life, and they are no longer so much at sea.

Ken: I like these questions. Not only do they externalize the voices, but they raise the question of whether or not they support opinions that are favoured by the person, or some other opinion that is different, and often opposed to the one that is preferred. One of the things that I find attractive about your work and writing is the attention you pay to relational politics and the techniques of power. Do you see a place for putting these ideas to work here?

Michael: Definitely. Exposing and describing the tactics that the voices employ to achieve what they achieve can be very helpful. These tactics can include all of those that make possible the privileging of one knowledge above others. And, when the chips are down, when their authority is at risk, these tactics also include various forms of abuse, terrorisation, subterfuge, treachery, pettiness, and so on.

Ken: That's interesting. Just how far are you willing to go, or how far are you prepared to extend, this re-voicing of the problem?

Michael: To reiterate, these voices rely upon time-honoured and disembodied speech acts for their influence. They draw attention to the motives of others, while disguising their own. In going to some lengths in the personifying of the voices, we open the possibilities for the deconstruction of, and unmasking of, all of this. In rendering transparent the voices' purposes in this way, people are assisted to revise their relationship with their voices. This personification also makes it more possible for us to assist people to monitor the progress of this revision in their relationship with their voices:

- *At this very moment, how are the voices coping with this exposure? To speak of them in this way, to unmask them in broad daylight, how does this affect them? Do you think that this is playing a part in reducing their influence, or playing a part in increasing this?*
- *Are the voices protesting this discussion? Has this unsettled them? Is this threatening to them? How are they reacting to the threat? Are they trying to "up the ante"? What do you think it means that they are threatened by this conversation?*
- *What is it like for the voices to have to listen to your thoughts for a change? What is it like for them to know that you are developing a disrespect for them and a mistrust of them - that you are on to their tricks of persuasion? How does this affect your position in your own life? Does it strengthen it, or weaken it?*

And so on.

Ken: Have others found these practices to be rather unusual?

Michael: Yes. And, as well, I want to be transparent about the fact that these practices have, as I have already mentioned, aroused some concerns. It has been said that I am somehow playing a role in the verification of what amounts to hallucinations, and thus culpable in the reinforcement of them. It has been argued that the problem with auditory hallucinations is that they are already externalized and that people need to own them, to integrate them - that the voices of schizophrenia really represent parts of the person that the person needs to integrate, thoughts that the person needs to come to terms with as their own, and so on. But these criticisms are based on modern notions of a "self" that is the centre of and source of all meaning, on notions of a unitary and essential self. And I do not believe that there is any hope whatsoever of sustaining this modern notion of the self.

Ken: So, if I understand you correctly, you encourage people to confront the voices. Does this ever take a form of the two-chair work that is common to Gestalt approaches?

Michael: No, definitely not. I am proposing something that is on the other side of these approaches - on the other side of such approaches at the levels of ideas, purpose, and practice. As I have said, the work to which I am referring is definitely not informed by the modern notions of the self, or by fashionable cultural notions about states of "wholeness" that might be achieved through "integration".

And there is no confrontation. Situations of direct conflict with these voices are avoided. In the practices that I am outlining in this discussion, there are no stand-offs. Highly emotive and stressful interactions are never encouraged. This would be entirely counter-productive. Rather, this work encourages people to take up an observer or self-reflexive position in relation to their own lives, a position in which they become the narrator of events in their relationship with the voices. Initially, this assists people to "suss out" the voices, and engages them in piecing together an exposé.

Ken: So, rather than integrating the so-called "split-off" parts of a single "self", as we might see in Gestalt approaches or even psychoanalytic approaches, you seem to be working to exclude the voices from people's lives.

Michael: The goal of this work is not to get rid of the hostile voices, but to assist people to revise their relationship with them, so that the voices' degree of influence is lessened. When people are in the subject position in regard to hostile voices, we can predict a deteriorating or relapsing course. When people break from the subject position, or when the voices are entered into the subject position, then we can predict improvements in the quality of people's lives, and fewer relapses.

However, as this work proceeds, it is not at all unusual for people to begin to report that the hostile voices absent themselves from their lives for significant periods. Because this is not an explicit goal, this sort of outcome is responded to as one of the bonuses of this work.

Ken: Back to what you were saying about confrontation, aren't there any occasions upon which direct confrontation would be indicated or useful?

Michael: Very rarely, and even then this would not take the form of a fight or a contest. Of course, at times people experience a strong temptation to enter the fray when they are experiencing the voices tantrumming, particularly when this is precipitated by a threat to the voices' position - when there is a chance that the voices might lose their "foothold" in their subject's life. But people are not encouraged to reciprocate. Instead, they stand back, consult their documents of identity or read transcripts of therapy sessions, and let these tantrums play themselves out. It is from this position, outside of the fray, that people become aware of various options for resistance.

Ken: You mentioned earlier that it can be helpful to assist persons to discriminate those voices that are supportive, or at least potentially supportive, from those voices that are hostile. Say more about this.

Michael: I believe that people who are subject to psychotic phenomena that are traumatising can do with all the support they can get, even if some of this support is to be found within the psychotic experience itself. It is not unusual for people in these circumstances to report that some of the voices they experience seem genuinely concerned for their wellbeing, even if they are at times somewhat misguided in their attempts to demonstrate this concern. Now, it is possible to assist people to more clearly distinguish these friendly or potentially friendly voices from the hostile voices, and to develop a stronger alliance with these more supportive voices, one in which they become better informed about what is in the person's best interest.

Such alliances can play a significant role in that they provide people with support and with the experience of a solidarity of purpose. This renders them less vulnerable to the insecurity that the hostile or dominating voices provoke and rely upon to achieve a position of influence in the person's life.

Ken: How do people go about developing a stronger alliance with the more supportive voices?

Michael: Well, after the identification of those voices that are friendly, or at least potentially friendly, people can be assisted to elaborate on the character of these to the point that they take on the identity of an invisible friend.

Ken: And when they can say something about the character of the friendly voice, the voice takes on greater depth and complexity, and is able to be more easily sustained and adopted. Would you say this is a key part of this work?

Michael: No. It is simply helpful, but by no means essential. And, of course, there are many people who do not experience such friendly or potentially friendly voices.

Ken: Are there any other ways that alliances could be developed which would help people who are vulnerable to hostile voices, say, for people who do not experience friendly or even potentially friendly voices?

Michael: Many. For example, we can explore the possibilities for the generation of relationships with invisible friends. It is possible to work with people around the invention of an invisible friend, and at times it is even possible to resurrect people's relationships with invisible friends. Do you have any idea of how many children have friendships with invisible friends? Children are generally more postmodern than adults in that they have a stronger appreciation of the multi-storied nature of personhood. Just ask around. Ask children, or ask some of your adult relatives or friends about whether they had invisible friends in childhood. You will be surprised at the prevalence of these friendships. And do you have any idea of what a difference friendships with invisible friends make to children's lives?

Ken: It's not something that I think a whole lot about.

Michael: Neither did I, but some years ago, in response to a conversation with Cheryl White about invisible friends, I began to ask people questions about this. As Cheryl had predicted, I was surprised by the responses I received.

Ken: I guess that they provide support and reassurance, cure loneliness, and so on.

Michael: You can also pass the buck to them when things get tough. And invisible friends do more than all these things. They are very empathic and compassionate, and are prepared to go through all manner of experiences with children, even to join children in suffering. I am sure that you have heard of children getting a great deal of solace from being joined in illness by invisible friends. Invisible friends make it so much easier for children to take the things that they have to take. And children can tell invisible friends secrets and, in so doing, give themselves a voice in this adult world where there is so little space given to children's voices.

Ken: I'm reminded of a popular comic strip here in the United States, *Calvin and Hobbes* - about a boy, Calvin, who is about six or seven years old, and his stuffed tiger, Hobbes, who is quite animated and lively, and plays a significant part in Calvin's life. How do you connect these ideas to your work on helping people revise their relationship with the voices heard in schizophrenia?

Michael: In this culture, at a certain point, children get talked out of their relationship with their invisible friends. This is considered to be developmentally-appropriate. However, I do keep in mind that there are many cultures in which a person's relationship with the equivalent of invisible friends is preserved, and in which their ongoing contribution to the person's life is acknowledged.

In my work with people who are harassed by the voices of schizophrenia, I sometimes learn of a childhood relationship with an invisible friend. I can then ask these people questions about what these invisible friends meant to them, about how these invisible friends contributed to their lives in ways that were sustaining, about the circumstances of the loss of this relationship, and so on. I can ask people questions about what they think it was that they brought to the invisible friend's life, and to speculate about what the separation meant to the invisible friend. We can then explore the possibilities for reunion, and talk about how such a reunion might be empowering to both parties. And then we can put together plans for the reunion. I have attended many such reunions, and have found them to be very moving and "warming" occasions.

Following these reunions, people can get their heads together with their invisible friends and document the hostile voices' usual habits of speech and action, develop predictions in regard to future attempts of these voices to establish supremacy, work on plans for how they might respond to this as a team, and so on.

Ken: Sounds fascinating! Although we have been mostly focussed on schizophrenia, I can see how these ideas have relevance to many other so-called psychiatric disorders.

Michael: They do. For example, take persons who are diagnosed with bipolar depression. We can engage these persons in externalizing conversations that have the effect of deconstructing both the grandiose ideas and the voice of depression. In the process, these people experience a degree of alienation in relation to these ideas and these voices, find that they are more able to monitor their emotional status, develop early intervention skills in reclaiming their lives from the destabilising effects of these ideas and voices, and become less vulnerable to acute episodes. But this is another story.

Ken: In the original interview I asked you about your theory on health/normality. In response, you said:

> *I think that all theories of health and normality are somewhat problematic because, regardless of their origins, they all wind up specifying lives and relationships, and all are entered into, albeit mostly inadvertently, in the service of subjugation. It is not possible to have a theory of normality without a positivist view and a utopian notion, and I do not believe that this can be sustained. A brief reflection on the history of ideas of health/normality is very discouraging of these ideas.*

So the work that you are talking about stands outside of most of the established conceptions of health and normality?

Michael: I believe that it does. But in some ways it is very helpful for us to know what the ideas and the practices of these notions of health and normality are. Upon identifying and clarifying these ideas and these practices, as well as the purposes to which they are put, people find themselves in a better position to determine possibilities for resisting what these notions incite them to do to their lives.

This knowledge also makes it possible for us to join with people in an exploration of those aspects of their life that they might be able to appreciate but that don't fit with these notions of health and normality. As some of these aspects become more visible to people, and as they become more embracing of these aspects, they are more able to honour their refusal to subject their lives to the ideas and practices that are informed by dominant notions of health and normality.

Ken: What is so important about the identification of and the honouring of this refusal?

Michael: Many of the people whom I meet who have a history of "schizophrenia" perceive themselves to have failed rather spectacularly in their attempts to be a person; that is, in their attempts to approximate the ways of being that are informed by dominant notions of health and normality. Other people in the community perceive this to constitute failure as well, and thus contribute to the sense of otherness and the marginalisation that is so keenly experienced by people who have histories of "schizophrenia", "manic depressive illness", and so on.

In response to all of this, many people who have psychiatric diagnoses wind up missing out on the small grant of moral worth that is accorded to others in our communities, and, as well, they give themselves a particularly hard time over not "making it". As if this isn't stressful enough, they so often go on to subject themselves to a great deal of pressure in their attempts to craft their life according to what these notions of health and normality specify. They wind up perpetually "stretched". These are the sort of circumstances that are favourable to acute episodes.

Ken: In some ways, we all get caught up in evaluating our lives on healthy/ sick, normal/abnormal continuums.

Michael: Yes. But many of us have a much greater chance of approximating those ways of being that are defined as healthy and normal than do others. Many of us are relatively successful at torturing ourselves into a state of "authenticity" and, in so doing, reproducing the "individuality" that is so venerated in this culture - although we all secretly know that we are not quite as together in regard to all of this as we appear to be to the world. But, psychotic expressions present an anathema to those cultural ways of being that we refer to as "self-possessed", "self-contained", "self-actualised", and so on. Psychotic experience, in this culture, rules people out of contention in the stakes for the achievement of personhood.

Ken: So you have talked about working with people in the honouring of the aspects of their life that they can appreciate and that don't fit with the dominant notions of health and normality. You have also talked about the importance of interpreting these aspects in ways that make it possible for them to be read as forms of refusal or as acts of resistance. Does this reopen the "stakes for personhood" as you would say it?

Michael: Yes it does. Stakes in the achievement of alternative versions of what it means to be a person.

Ken: Do externalizing conversations come into this?

Michael: They do. For example, the various ideas and practices that are associated with dominant notions of health and normality can be externalized as "expectations" and "ambitions". The requirements of these expectations and ambitions, their various incitements, and, as well, the terms that they dictate for people's lives, can be explored. This enables people to separate their lives and their identities from these ideas and practices, and opens space for what had previously been interpreted as failure to be reinterpreted as resistance or protest. In breaking their lives from those ways of being that are informed by dominant notions of health and normality, people experience a freedom to explore other ways of being in the world.

Ken: Having this kind of freedom to explore other ways of being would probably reduce a lot of stress in these people's lives - and maybe even their vulnerability to future acute episodes.

Michael: Very significantly.

Ken: These externalizing conversations are generated through a process of questioning?

Michael: Yes. This questioning process is maintained throughout this work, even in relation to those events that people read as progress. For example: *Are you doing this at a pace that suits the expectations, or at a pace that suits you?*

Ken: In *Narrative Means to Therapeutic Ends*, you and David Epston provided many examples of therapeutic letters and other documents that assist people to re-author their lives according to preferred stories. Do you use letters and documents in this work as well?

Michael: Most certainly. In times of stress - when we find ourselves under significant duress when facing situations of adversity - we are all vulnerable to being separated from our knowledgeableness. At these times, we often experience a dearth of creative responses to the situations we find ourselves in; our usual problem-solving skills don't seem available to us, and our options for action seem to evaporate. Our focus of attention can become very narrow, we can begin to lose our sense of identity and, at times, when the stress that we are subject to is particularly acute, we can undergo something akin to paralysis.

Now, those people who have experienced psychotic episodes are ever so much more vulnerable to being dispossessed of their knowledgeableness and their preferred sense of identity at such times. And it is this dispossession that sets the scene for the experience of great personal insecurity and distress, and for further acute episodes. So it makes a great deal of sense for these people to carry with them, at all times, documents of their identity. These are documents that they can consult under those circumstances when they are losing sight of their knowledgeableness, when their sense of identity is at risk.

Ken: What do these documents look like?

Michael: There are many aspects to these documents, and many possible forms. Such documents can include some historical account of the person's ability to intervene, on his or her own behalf, in his/her own life. This is an account of personal agency, an account that emphasises what could be called the person's "agentive self". It includes details about what the person has been up against in the performance of this personal agency, and, against this background, emphasises the significance of any more recent steps that the person has been taking toward having more to say about how their life goes.

These documents are grounded in hope; for example, they often include details about the sort of personal qualities and other characteristics that were available to the person in the earlier years of their life, and speculation about how, when, and under what circumstances these might resurface in the service of the person's own plans and goals. These documents can also include details about any recent developments in the person's problem-solving skills.

Because other people's responses to the sort of identity claims that are reflected in these documents are of critical importance, those people who might provide an appropriate audience to this alternative account of the person's identity are specifically referred to in these documents. This is achieved in a way that is less likely to leave the response of this audience to chance - the wording is put in such a way as to invite acknowledging responses from this audience.

These documents are ever available to the person to consult, and are particularly valuable to them at times of stress and during crises. These are the times at which the person concerned is at risk of being dispossessed of their knowledgeableness. To facilitate this consultation, these documents usually include a self-referencing paragraph, one that further disempowers the voices through exposé, and one that invites the person to respond to crises with further revisions of their relationships with their voices. But this is not all, and perhaps I could here include an example of one of these documents.

Bev gave permission for this document to be reproduced here on the understanding that this might contribute to possibilities for others who experience voices. As she would be interested in feedback about whether

Document of Bev's Identity

In the past week, in the face of great odds, Bev was able to hang in, and, in confronting a great challenge, she found the resources to rise to the occasion. In this way she eventually got the upper hand, and reclaimed the territory of her own life. For passing this significant test, Bev gave herself six out of ten, Michael gave her seven out of ten, and Rosie gave her seven out of ten (Bev had requested this assessment).

Upon reflecting on this achievement to determine what sort of personal qualities Bev was depending upon, those of PATIENCE and STRENGTH came immediately to mind. These qualities have been available to Bev historically, and she has relied upon them to see her though difficult times. The fact that they are resurfacing now is cause for celebration.

There were other qualities that were available to Bev historically, and these include FORTITUDE, COURAGE, RESILIENCE, and STAMINA. It could be expected that these will also resurface and that Bev will be able to put them to work in further challenges to the fake authority of the voices. All of the qualities mentioned so far would be appreciated by Bev's mother, father, and two sisters.

In addition to this, recent events suggest the development of some entirely new personal skills. These are in the area of REACHING-OUT, SELF-APPRECIATION, and SELF-EMBRACING. Bev's mother and her sisters would be delighted with this news, and would recognise the significance of this personal achievement.

There are developments that also suggest that Bev is breaking from the grief that she has held for so long in relation to her father's death. This is significant because she realises that her father's image should be important, but that it should not dominate her life.

Because the truth is very disempowering of hostile voices, whenever they try to hassle Bev she will read this document to them. This will confront them with their deceit and the petty nature of their claims, and will provoke them to take a back seat in her life.

this turned out to be the case, if appropriate, readers of this transcript might consider writing to her, c/-Dulwich Centre.

This document of identity was shaped by Bev's requirements, and they do not always take this form - for example, they can be set out in a series of points.

Ken: You said that these documents are always available for consultation?

Michael: Yes. It is not uncommon for the people who consult me to carry several documents of this sort on their person at all times. This way, they are ever available to be consulted. This considerably alleviates people's anxiety in the face of the trials and tribulations of everyday existence, and renders them less vulnerable to acute episodes.

Ken: It seems that a lot of the ideas and practices that you are talking about here would really help reduce the possibility that people will think of themselves as failures. They have on-hand written proof of an alternative story of their lives. Still, I wonder what happens when they are in such an acute crisis that hospitalisation is needed. What then?

Michael: You are right about the emphasis that I place on reducing the possibility that people will perceive themselves as failures. In our culture, the opportunities to experience failure are boundless and are ever-available. And, as already discussed, some people are more vulnerable to this than others and, for them, the experience of failure very significantly increases their vulnerability to what is often referred to as relapses. This has devastating consequences to their quality of life and to their course in life generally.

In the light of this, it makes sense for us to make it our business to ensure that the contexts of our work are structured to reduce the possibility that people might read failure into their responses to the world. This should be as true for the context of hospitalisation as it is for any other context. Unfortunately, however, the receiving frame that is in place for most admissions to psychiatric hospitals is one that reads the events that precipitate hospitalisation as regress. People are admitted as a result of having "breaks", because they are "decompensating", and so on. Upon admission to hospital, the events of people's lives are interpreted in ways that give rise to mostly negative connotations. To interpret the crises that precipitate admission to hospital as regress contributes significantly to despair, demoralisation and, of course, to distress - for those people who are being admitted, and for those who are in family, kinship, and friendship networks. Relatives and friends often experience feelings of inadequacy over not having "done better" in supporting the person who is admitted to hospital, and it is not at all unusual for them to experience substantial guilt at these times. As well, the negative connotations that are associated with hospital admission fuel, for everybody concerned, a sense of hopelessness about the future, and a personal dread that is based on predictions about the draining nature of the experiences that they have ahead of them in their relationship with the person who is being admitted. So, interpreting the crises that precipitate admission as regressive has profoundly negative effects on the lives and the relationships of all concerned.

Ken: But in proposing an alternative story about admission to the hospital, you are not suggesting that hospitalisation be understood as something to celebrate, are you?

Michael: No, definitely not. And at these times of crises it is important that people's distress be appropriately acknowledged. But I believe that the sense of failure, and the associated experiences of despair and demoralisation that are so often the outcome of these sort of admissions to hospital, are far from inevitable. In fact I believe that these experiences are mostly avoidable. We can establish different receiving frames for these admissions, ones that inform alternative interpretations of the crises that precipitate admission, ones that shape more positive outcomes for all involved - ones that undermine the possibilities for people to experience despair, demoralisation and a sense of failure under these circumstances.

So, it turns out that while people's experiences of distress associated with the events leading up to hospitalisation, and over the hospitalisation itself, can be powerfully acknowledged, the meanings associated with such admissions are open to negotiation. In fact, regardless of the situation, these meanings are always negotiated, and the particular meanings that are derived from this have an entirely significant effect on the outcome.

Ken: What is an example of one of these alternative receiving frames that you are referring to?

Michael: The "rite of passage" metaphor provides such a frame[1]. My understanding of this metaphor is derived from the work of the anthropologists van Gennep (1960) and Turner (1969). According to this work, there are three phases to the rites of passage that facilitate transitions in life. These are the "separation" phase, the "liminal" or "betwixt-and-between" phase, and the "reincorporation" phase.

I don't believe that this is the place to review in detail the work of these anthropologists, which is mostly about the structures that facilitate transitions in people's lives in traditional cultures. So, I will restrict myself to just a few comments about their rite of passage metaphor.

According to this metaphor, the first phase of a rite of passage facilitates, through communal ritual process, a novice's separation or detachment from a particular status and location in the social order - or, if you like, from a particular "state" of life. In the second phase, the novice enters a space that is between known worlds, one in which nothing is as it was, one that features a primary condition of ambiguity, one in which considerable confusion and disorientation are to be experienced. Everything that the novice had previously taken for granted can no longer be taken so. Then, after a period of time, it is deemed that the novice is ready to rejoin the familiar world, but at a different location in the social order, one that brings with it new responsibilities and freedoms, new habits of thought and action. This is the reincorporation phase, and in traditional cultures it is marked by community acknowledgement through ceremony. The novice is a novice no longer, and has arrived at a position in life that was not

---

1. This metaphor has been employed by others for similar purposes in modifying the receiving frames for admission to residential care facilities (see Menses & Durrant 1986).

available to them beforehand. Communal acknowledgement plays an entirely significant role in the confirmation of, and authentication of, the new identity claims that are associated with reincorporation.

If we were to take this metaphor as a receiving frame for hospitalisation, then admission would be renamed discharge, and discharge would be renamed admission. At the point of hospitalisation it can be assumed that the person is being discharged from a particular status or location in the social world that was no longer appropriate for them to occupy, and this would inform a series of questions about what the person might be separating from in terms of expectations, roles, responsibilities, duties, obligations, habits of thought and action, affiliations, particular circumstances or conditions of life, etc. - that, for whatever reason, are no longer appropriate or acceptable. As stress is a significant feature in the precipitation of acute episodes, then many of these questions can be oriented to the identification of what might have been stressing of the person's life, of what had been stretching them beyond what was appropriate for them.

Questions of the sort that I am referring to here can be addressed at a meeting of family and friends around the time of admission. At times, the person who is undergoing the acute crisis is not able to be "present" for such a meeting, and in these circumstances the speculative responses to these questions can be checked out with the person at the point at which they become more "available".

Ken: I would guess that the rite of passage metaphor as you use it here could make a significant difference in the way that people might understand their hospitalisation and "inpatient" phase.

Michael: This metaphor provides for a reinterpretation of the confusion and disorientation that is almost routinely experienced by people at these times of crisis, for it proposes that the "inpatient" phase is a liminal or betwixt-and-between phase. People can come to an appreciation of the fact that there is always some distance between the point of separation from something, and the point of arrival at something else, and that in this space it is only reasonable to expect a very considerable degree of confusion and disorientation. Within the context of this receiving frame, these experiences cease to be read as regress, but as the virtual inevitable outcome of journeying to a new place in life.

To facilitate this reading of experience during the period of admission, staff can spend time with the person and members of his/her kinship and friendship networks over (a) further speculation about what the person might be separating from, (b) what circumstances of life might be more suitable for him/her and more favourable to quality of life, and (c) the investigation of any clues that might provide some thoughts about the ways of life that might be available for the person to step into at the completion of this particular transition.

Ken: And I suppose that the discharge from hospital would be the "reincorporation phase"?

Michael: Yes. Family, friends, acquaintances, staff, and so on, can be invited to another gathering which is described as the re-admission meeting. At this meeting, an opportunity is provided for the person to speak as an authority on their own life and to give an account of their journey, one that includes information about what this has clarified for them in regard to the circumstances of life that would favour quality of life, and that would suit them better personally. In this context, the others who are present are encouraged to respond in ways that are acknowledging of the person's status as an authority on his/her life, of the person's knowledgeableness. As well, all of those present at these gatherings are encouraged to explore any alterations that might be necessary in their relationships to the person in order to accommodate these changes.

Ken: How does this affect the course of hospitalisations that many people are going through?

Michael: On those occasions that I have been able to structure this sort of receiving context, which is nowhere near as often as I would have liked, it has definitely had the effect of reducing the length and number of hospital admissions. But the sample is small, and I have not had the opportunity to follow this up further in recent years.

What is most important about establishing this alternative receiving frame is that people learn to read their experiences of distress and confusion differently. And this even makes it possible for them to respond differently to their milder experiences of psychotic phenomena - those that do not precipitate hospitalisation. These experiences come to signify a liminal phase that opens the possibility for people to take further steps to determine a lifestyle that would suit them. This very significantly undermines the despair, insecurity, and panic, which are all complicating in the sense that they intensify the psychotic experience. In the place of this despair, insecurity, and panic, we see the development of a certain sense of curiosity about the outcome of the transition, and of the sort of hope that helps people through these crises.

Ken: What about future hospitalisations? Would they tend to undermine the validity of this rite of passage metaphor?

Michael: Not if these are predicted, which they reasonably can be. The idea that life is comprised of a series of transitions is not at all novel in our culture. And it can be openly assumed that the people who have experienced hospitalisation in a context that is informed by the rite of passage metaphor are likely to go through further transitions marked by the phases of separation, liminality and reincorporation. And if the circumstances of these hospitalisations are favourable, this turns out to be not such a bad context for the negotiation of these liminal phases of a person's life.

So, when people have a history of many and frequent admissions, at times it makes lots of sense to sit down and talk with them about the wisdom of scheduling future admissions in advance of psychotic episodes. This scheduling can be determined by reviewing previous admissions to determine the average time elapsed between admissions, and by bringing the scheduled admission ahead of this by a slim margin.

Ken: So, what happens during these subsequent admissions? How are they structured?

Michael: In exactly the same way as those we have already discussed. The admission is seen as an opportunity to take time out to review one's life to determine which aspects of it might be incompatible with those ways of life that the person is most suited to. This provides for people the opportunity to identify what circumstances of life might be stressing of them, and which of these circumstances they might be ready to break their lives from.

Ken: So this doesn't mean that the person winds up being hospitalised more often?

Michael: The therapeutic practices that we have been reviewing throughout this interview all have the potential to reduce admissions to hospital. And this is no less true for the practice of scheduled admissions that I am describing. The sort of admissions that I am proposing actually work against acute episodes. And, as people experience fewer disabling episodes, they begin to modify the schedule by reducing the length of admissions and by stretching the interval between admissions.

Ken: How realistic is it to believe that institutions like psychiatric hospitals are going to be interested and able to do what amounts to turning their procedures upside down?

Michael: I think that the potential to achieve this is significant. There are many administrators and clinical directors out there who are looking for some viable alternatives to the established practices of hospitalisation, alternatives that are likely to contribute to the quality of life of the people who are the recipients of their services, and alternatives that are likely to deal with the high levels of malaise and demoralisation experienced by the staff of these institutions.

Ken: In this country [USA] insurance companies are having a lot more to say about treatment generally, including hospital admissions and the length of admissions. What happens to the possibilities to practice what you are suggesting under such circumstances?

Michael: I don't really know enough about the "ins" and the "outs" of what is happening here to comment much. Obviously what I am proposing here could be as much in the interests of insurance companies as it is in everybody else's interest. But I don't know how well wisdom sits with insurance companies.

Ken: Throughout this interview, your responses to my questions have conveyed a strong sense of the possibilities that are available to mental health professionals in this work. But what are the options for mental health professionals who want to take up the sort of possibilities that you have outlined in this interview, but who do not have the backing of their institutions, and who are not in positions of significant power?

Michael: Rarely do the institutions of our culture succeed in establishing states of pure domination. Because of this, in most institutions, spaces or gaps can be found through which workers can express their moral agency. And, in stepping into these gaps, we can all play a role in the transformation of the institutions that we work for.

We can ignore the arbitrary boundaries of these institutions, and we can go out and meet with people and encourage them to draw distinctions around which ways of speaking about their lives are respectful and honouring of their knowledges, and which ways of speaking about their lives are marginalising and disqualifying of this knowledgeableness. We can join with people in developing ideas for informing the institutions of this, and for recruiting the active participation of these institutions in the further development of practices that these people consider more personally empowering. I have seen those people who are the "consumers" of psychiatric services enter into this educative role with a great deal of benevolence and empathy for the staff of the institutions concerned.

Ken: This has been rather a long interview, and perhaps we should draw it to a close. Would you like to make some parting comments?

Michael: Yes. despite the length of this interview, what we have been talking about is a partial account of this work. There are many other considerations.

Ken: Any that you would like to briefly name here.

Michael: Yes. The provision of appropriate community support to people with psychiatric diagnoses is a consideration of critical importance. For those readers who want to review this dimension, and who haven't yet begun, I would suggest consulting Chris Beels' "Invisible Village" (1989). It is a great starting point.

Ken: I've really enjoyed this interview, Michael. I think a lot of what you have said really challenges the ways in which so-called psychiatric patients have been labelled, shunned, categorised, written-off, and otherwise marginalised, or, in your own words, subjugated - and the use of this term gives the whole process a more political flavour - which is what you have so refreshingly brought to our attention. Thank you.

Michael: And I've enjoyed this opportunity to renew my contact with you, and to further discuss this work.

REFERENCES

Beels, C.C. 1989:
"The invisible village." In Beels, C.C. & Bachrach, L.L. (Eds), "Survival strategies for `public psychiatry", Vol.42 (Summer, pp.27-40) of **New Directions for Mental Health Services**. San Francisco: Jossey-Bass.

Menses, G. & Durrant, M. 1986:
"Contextual residential care." **Dulwich Centre Review**. Adelaide: Dulwich Centre Publications.

Turner, V. 1969:
The Ritual Process. New York: Cornell University Press.

van Gennep, A. 1960:
The Rites of Passage. Chicago: University of Chicago Press.

6.   A Conversation About Accountability*
*Interviewer: Christopher McLean***

Chris: Michael, I'm interested in exploring your ideas about the implications of accountability for therapy. I am particularly interested in how you are actually working with these concepts, and how they might extend the work that you are doing.

Michael: In response to this question, I would like to focus mainly on the work that I've been doing with men who abuse. Even when the partners and children of these men are looking for reconciliation, in the first place it is my practice to see these men alone. This greatly facilitates the achievement of some of the preliminary tasks, and this in turn helps to set the scene for the introduction of processes of accountability.

Chris: What are these preliminary tasks?

Michael: Well, apart from taking the necessary steps to secure the safety of their women partners and their children, the sort of tasks that men who have abused are faced with at this time have to do with:

---

*   Previously published 1994 in "Dulwich Centre Newsletter", Nos.2&3.

**   Christopher McLean can be contacted c/- Dulwich Centre Publications.

(a) taking responsibility for perpetrating the abuse,

(b) developing an understanding of the experiences of those who have been subject to the abuse, and

(c) establishing a thorough appreciation of the short-term effects of the abuse, and also of the possible longer-term effects of this abuse on the lives of those who were subject to it, should there be an absence of redress.

It is also important to allocate sufficient time to work with these men to help them in the development of an apology that is congruent with the steps they have made in taking responsibility for perpetrating the abuse, and that is congruent with their understanding of the effects of the abuse on those who are subject to it. Many of these points have been addressed by Alan Jenkins in his book, *Invitations to Responsibility* (1990).

As part of the apology, when children have been abused it is important for men to provide an account of how they have managed to intimidate the non-abusive parent into silence and inaction, or an account of the power tactics that they relied upon to maintain secrecy around the abuse. This goes some way towards mending the relationship between children and the non-offending parent. This is important, because this relationship is so often one of the casualties of the abuse.

Chris: Can you say something about why it's important to meet alone in the beginning? Is that related to these ideas of accountability?

Michael: Yes, it is related to certain ideas about accountability. It's important that we get together as men and speak with our own voices against the abuse, and not just rely on the voices of those who have been subject to the abuse. And, as well, for men to rely upon those people who have been subject to the abuse to spell out the effects of the abuse on their lives is to heap one injustice upon another. To do this is further burdening of those people who have been subject to the abuse.

Chris: So how do you actually go about helping men gain an understanding of the effects of their actions?

Michael: There are many ways of doing this. Perhaps I could briefly discuss one of these.

Quite a number of these men have been subject to abuse in their own lives, in their own families of origin, and also in their peer relationships with other men. And all have some experiences of abuse, although not necessarily physical, in the various institutions of our culture. Initially these men tend to minimise the significance of that abuse in their own lives. But engaging them in some exploration of the effects of abuses that they have been subject to in their own lives, including experiences of institutional humiliation and degradation, is important. Often it's only when men attend carefully to the effects of some of these experiences of abuse that they actually reach a point where they can name abuse for what it is, and appreciate the full impact of the violence that they have perpetrated on others.

Chris: How do you feel confident that this understanding has actually been integrated and that the perpetrator is not simply saying those things that he knows you want him to say?

Michael: I think this understanding is only something that can be developed, or reached, within the context of the interaction with these men. This occurs as part of a process, and it would be very hard for me to just talk about one or two signs that may provide some sense of security that this understanding has been achieved.

However, I will say that what I often witness during the course of this work is the expression of a great deal of distress when these men, for the first time, get in touch with the real effects of this abuse in the lives of their women partners or children. Perhaps this is one sign that gives me a sense that this understanding is being achieved.

And I do think that it is possible to draw a distinction around a "performance" of remorse on the one hand, and, on the other, the expression of the distress that these men experience upon some realisation of the fact of what they have done.

Chris: My understanding is that you believe it is important for the male therapist not to speak from a separate or morally superior position. That is, the therapist needs to make it clear to the client that he sees himself as being basically part of the same culture from which the abuse has taken place, enabling some sort of joining to happen. Have I understood you correctly in that?

Michael: Yes. In this work with men who abuse, we talk about our experiences of men's culture. But it's not just about joining. When I meet with men who have perpetrated violence, I cannot afford to see them as aberrant. To see them as aberrant, to regard them as "other", would enable me to obscure the link between the violence of these men and the dominant ways of being and thinking for men in this culture that venerate aggression, domination, and conquest.

To see them as aberrant would enable me, as a man, to avoid confronting the ways that I might be complicit in the reproduction of these dominant ways of being and thinking.

To see these men who perpetrate violence as aberrant would enable me, as a member of the class of men, to avoid facing the responsibility that I have to take action to contribute to the dismantling of men's privilege that perpetuates inequality of opportunity, and that supports domination.

To see these men who perpetrate violence as aberrant would enable me to avoid taking action to play a part in destabilising the structures of oppression, and to avoid challenging the practices of power that are subjugating of and marginalising of others. And it would enable me to continue to leave it to those people in the least powerful position to raise issues of disqualification, exploitation, abuse, and so on, and to continue to leave it to these people to take action to end this. For me to see these men as aberrant would be all too convenient, a "cop-out".

Chris: So, when you're working with a violent man, you also have a personal accountability towards the victim of the man's abuse, because of your own involvement in that same culture.

Michael: That's correct. I do believe that I am personally accountable, and I'm very interested in how this whole context of therapy might be structured so that I might be confronted with the special responsibilities that are associated with this accountability.

Chris: I'd like to ask you about a view that I have heard, which asserts that violent and abusive men never really change "deep down", and that they simply learn, at best, that the consequences of further abuse are such that they have to control their actions.

Michael: Well, I think that a lot of the work that is carried out with men who are abusive stops short; so often it stops at a point where the work is only half done, and frequently at a point where it isn't even half done.

It's really not enough for these men to just take responsibility for the abuse. It's not enough for them to make it their business to get in touch with the experiences of this abuse. It's not enough for these men to identify the short-term and possible longer-term consequences of this. It's not enough for them to develop an appropriate apology. It's not enough for them to enter into some commitment to mend what might be mended. And it is not enough for them to do all of this and to confront the patriarchal ways of thinking and being that inform the abuse.

It is important to establish a context in which it becomes possible for these men to separate from some of the dominant ways of being and thinking that inform the abuse. These are those ways of being and thinking that inform, support, justify, and make the abuse possible. But even this is not enough. It is crucial that we engage with these men in the exploration of alternative ways of being and thinking that bring with them new proposals for action in their relationships with their women partners and with their children, and that these proposals be accountable to these women and children.

To achieve this, the specifics of these alternative ways of being and thinking need to be very carefully worked through. The particularities of any proposals for these alternative ways of being and thinking must be carefully drawn out.

Chris: So how do you actually go about enabling men to separate from practices which may be very deeply internalized?

Michael: I won't go into this in too much detail here, because it takes us away from the subject of accountability. But I will say that I involve these men in what I call externalizing conversations about the sorts of attitudes and beliefs that are used to justify domination and abuse, about the structures of domination that inform men's perpetration of abuse on the lives of women, children, and other men, about the sorts of techniques of power and control that make this possible, and so on. I explore with these men the extent to which their lives have been entered, and the extent to which they have entered their own lives, into the abusive ways of thinking and ways of being that are informed by all of this. We review the historical forces that have played a significant role in recruiting men into these ways of being and thinking. And, together, we explore the extent to which these ways of being and thinking have in fact shaped or constituted men's relationships with others generally, and the abusive man's relationship with his woman partner and his children more specifically.

It is in the process of these externalizing conversations that, often for the first time, men step away from the idea that these abusive ways of being speak of their nature, or speak to them of authentic ways of being as men in relation to women, children, and other men.

I then work with these men to identify some aspects of their relationships, or some aspects of their desires and purposes, that contradict these dominant and oppressive ways of being and thinking. There will always be some examples of the sort of interactions and purposes that stand outside of those that are informed by dominantly abusive ways of being, and these become points of entry for what I call re-authoring conversations. I have documented such conversations in some detail in various places, and I don't wish to do this again at this point. However, I will say that these contradictions become all the easier to identify the more extensively we explore together the real effects of these attitudes and tactics of power and control in the man's life, and the real effects of these on his relationships.

Chris: What does relate to accountability, I think, is the point that you've often made about how difficult it is for you as the therapist, and for the men themselves, to be completely sure that their proposals for new ways of being are not unwittingly reproducing dominant ways of being. This, surely, makes it particularly important that these proposals are accountable to the people who have experienced the abuse?

Michael: It is never possible for us, as men, to be secure in the idea that we are not inadvertently reproducing ways of being and thinking that might be experienced as dominating by those who have been in the subjugated position. We are of men's culture, and we can never wholly stand outside of it.

So, it's really important to establish a context that makes it possible for us to speak with these men about their proposals for alternative and preferred ways of being in their relationships, and at the same time to get feedback on these proposals from those who have been in the subject position. This is a context in which men, at a certain point, have the opportunity to be an audience to the responses of their women partners and their children.

This is a context of accountability in which it becomes possible for men to not just acknowledge responsibility for the abuse, and to not just share with those people who have been subject to abuse an understanding of the real effects of that abuse on their lives. It is a context in which men can also get feedback from women and children on the specifics of their proposals for future action, on their proposals for alternative ways of being with their partners and their children and other men. '

There is another piece to the accountability structures in this work. This is the establishment of contexts for men's accountability to other men, for men's accountability to each other. It's always important to assist men to locate and to meet with other men who are also exploring alternative ways of being and thinking for men. These forums make it possible for men to join their voices against those aspects of men's culture that are abusive, and provide support for men to renegotiate their proposals for alternative ways of being in the light of feedback that they are receiving from their partners and children. By creating contexts in which men can talk together about the likely consequences of failure to break from the abusive ways of being, and the likely consequences of achieving success in this, particularly in regard to the lives of women and children, and in regard to the men's relationships with these women and children, these forums assist men to come to terms with what is at stake in their respective projects. These forums are formed by men who might be acquaintances, friends, relatives, or by men whom I introduce to each other.

Chris: What you've just suggested about men locating other men could potentially lead to some kind of men's caucus. Who would you encourage to participate in forming a caucus for those who have been subject to abuse or violence?

Michael: What's happened in my practice to date is that I have met with those people who have been subject to the abuse, along with other members of their immediate family, and other relatives and friends who are supportive and non-violent. At these times we have discussed the importance of accountability, and, if reconciliation is on their agenda, I have explored their degree of willingness to play a role in a formal structure of accountability.

Are they interested and prepared to meet and to be an audience to the man's declaration of responsibility, his understanding of the experiences of the abuse, his apology, his proposal for mending what might be mended, and also his proposal for alternative and preferred ways of being in his relationships with his children and his partner?

If they agree to do this, then we can proceed on the understanding that it's not their responsibility to put the man in touch with their experiences of the abuse - it's just their prerogative to give the man feedback on his understandings. And it's not their responsibility to come up with, or take responsibility for, how the man should be in his relationships with women, children, and other men, but to give him feedback about his proposals, feedback about what they predict would be the effects of these proposals on their lives.

At a later point, if trust is established by the man's response to this, those who have been subject to the abuse become motivated to bear witness to their experiences of abuse in these structured contexts.

Chris: How might you extend on this in the light of the ideas on accountability developed by Kiwi Tamasese and Charles Waldegrave (1993)?

Michael: Well, in response to the work that The Family Centre have been doing, I am more aware of how important it is for there to be a wider caucusing for those people who have been in the subject position and for the non-abusive family members. So, I've been thinking about how I might actually get several families together for this process, so that the women and children of the families that I am meeting with get support from caucusing in a wider group.

Chris: So, can you foresee a situation where a man would declare his responsibility for the abuse he has perpetrated, and his proposals about changes, not just to the individual woman or child who has experienced the abuse, but in the presence of a caucus of people with similar experiences?

Michael: Yes, I think this could be very helpful. And, to an extent, this is already happening. I have argued (White 1991) that it is important that ongoing local accountability be structured into this work. One example of this is the institution of "escape-from-secrecy meetings". These meetings include the participation of a representative of those who have been subject to abuse. I think that this structure is particularly effective if this representative has had similar experiences of abuse, and has some consciousness of the gender politics that form the context of this.

But a greater familiarity with The Family Centre's notion of accountability structures has me thinking about the importance of a wider representation at the interface of accountability, as well as wider representation with regard to the actual caucusing. I know that I will be emphasising this more in the future.

Chris: Could you say something here about how you see yourself, as a man working in this area, being accountable to women who are also working with the victims of abuse?

Michael: I'm actually in a position to get a lot of feedback about my work. For many years I have been incorporating aspects of my work with men who abuse in workshops and other teaching contexts. At these times, I receive a lot of feedback about this work from responses to video-taped recordings of interviews. This feedback is invaluable to me and to the men, women and children who have agreed to the video-taping, and who are enthusiastic about playing some part in informing the professional community. I also receive feedback from women and men who work in the field and who directly observe some of my interviews. I continue to explore ways of making what I am doing as transparent as possible. So I do have quite an extensive system of accountability.

However, the work of The Family Centre draws my attention to the critical importance of establishing more formal accountability structures, and this has got me thinking about how I might establish this in my work, about how I might be able to make my work more formally accountable to those women who are working with the women and children who have been subject to abuse.

Chris: Can you say anything about the ideas that you've been considering?

Michael: I have been considering the idea of establishing some sort of forum that might be available to men who work with men who are violent. This would involve approaching women who work with women and children who have been subject to abuse, with a request that they contribute to such a forum along the lines of the accountability structures that are proposed by The Family Centre.

Chris: Do you think that the concept of accountability implies that men should only work with men in these circumstances, and that male therapists shouldn't work with women who have been the victims of abuse?

Michael: I'd be very concerned about any position that denies choice to those people who are seeking our help, and about any position that is determined by a consideration of rules rather than by a consideration of ethics. But I also I think that, as men, we have an imperative to share, with the women who consult us, what we see as the possible dangers of this, including the extent to which women's knowledges are so often disqualified in these contexts, and the possible limitations that might be associated with the fact of our gender. These limitations can be exposed in part by the therapist giving notice that, in the context of therapy, he will take responsibility for any misunderstanding or particular difficulties with achieving understanding, and will assume that these will relate considerably to the privilege that is associated with his location in the social world of gender.

Chris: So, it would be a situation where some kind of accountability structure would be particularly important.

Michael: Very important. But we can also ask those women who do choose to meet with us about how our work together might be made accountable to other women in their social networks. Invariably women are prepared to explore this with their relatives, friends and acquaintances. To find other women who have been subject to abuse, who might play a part in this, is particularly important.

So, what in effect happens in these circumstances is that the woman who is consulting me gets feedback from other women in regard to the woman's account of the work that is taking place between us. I believe that this is another very important piece to the general accountability process.

Chris: Can you elaborate on that a bit, and say what this means in practical terms?

Michael: Well, in practical terms, it involves me sharing with the woman some of my concerns, and asking some questions about any thoughts that she might have that could help to make my participation in the therapeutic interaction more accountable to other women. This might involve us talking about family, friendship, and acquaintanceship networks, about which women in these networks might be prepared to play this part, about how these women might be approached about this, and so on.

At times, the woman finds it helpful to video or audio-tape our meetings and to take this away to share with the other women who have agreed to contribute to this sort of accountability structure. And at times the woman invites these women to meet with us in our work together. This provides at least some check on the possibilities for the inadvertent reproduction of gender politics in the course of the work.

Chris: Is this something that you've actually tried yourself?

Michael: Yes. It's part of my practice, and has been for some time.

Chris: I'd like to ask you about accountability more generally between therapist and client. Given that accountability is about addressing power differences, how do you deal with the differences in power between you and the person who you are working with, apart from the specific gender issues that we have been discussing so far?

Michael: I think that this is a very important point. There is a power differential in the therapy context, and it is one that cannot be erased, regardless of how committed we are to egalitarian practices. Although there are many steps that we can take to render the therapeutic interaction more egalitarian, if we believe that we can arrive at some point at which we can interact with those people who seek our help in a way that is totally outside of any power relation, then we are treading on dangerous ground. Such a belief would enable us to avoid the moral and ethical responsibilities that we have to those people who seek our help, and that they don't have to us. And I don't think that we can ever afford to lose sight of that. To do so would serve to open up possibilities for the abuse and exploitation of those people who seek our help.

So some acknowledgement of this power differential is essential for this reason. And, as well, if we do acknowledge the fact of the inescapability of this power differential, then it is more likely that we will stay on the lookout for action that we can take to render the context of therapy more egalitarian, and we are more likely to persevere in our attempts to build in various forms of accountability that are ongoing through the process of the therapy itself.

Chris: I know that you have a particular attitude towards clients' casenotes that seems to me to be directly related to these ideas of accountability. Could you tell me about this?

Michael: Well, I have an ethical commitment to only record information in the presence of those people who are consulting me.

I believe that any recording of the discussion in interviews should be undertaken only within the presence of those people who are seeking our help, and that it should not be done outside of that context. It is also important that anything that gets written down should be transparent in that context of the therapeutic interaction.

If we do wish to record any details of the discussion that takes place within the therapeutic context, then I believe that we should routinely ask the permission of those people who are consulting us, and that we should clarify our purposes for recording such details. I make it my responsibility to read through what I am recording at the time of the recording, and invite the person with whom I am working to make appropriate amendments or corrections to these details. It is my position that any recording that we have permission to undertake in this context should be verbatim unless we explicitly negotiate other arrangements. And, unless otherwise negotiated, the ownership of the notes should reside with the people who consult us.

Chris: What do you see as being the real effects of the standard practice of keeping extensive casenotes that are not dealt with in this open and accountable way?

Michael: I think that what you are referring to as the standard practice of recording has the effect of pathologising and marginalising those people who seek our help. It is a practice that contributes significantly to their experience of "otherness", and one that reinforces some of the very negative stories of identity that are experienced by so many of these people. It is a practice that plays a significant part in modern rituals of degradation.

Chris: I've heard that one of your ways of establishing accountability procedures is, on occasion, to actually employ people who have been your clients to observe you and to comment on your work. Could you elaborate upon that?

Michael: I take very seriously the idea that this work is a two-way process. There is at large an idea that the sole recipients of therapy are those people who consult therapists. I think that this idea structures a therapy that is marginalising of those people who seek our help. It contributes further to the construction of these people as "other".

Thus, I have an ethical commitment to bring forth the extent to which the process of therapy is a two-way process, and to try to find ways of identifying, acknowledging, and articulating the extent to which the therapeutic interactions are actually shaping of the work itself, and also shaping of my life more generally in positive ways. This includes acknowledging the extent to which this work is inspiring of many further developments.

But we can go further in the acknowledgement of the extent to which this work is a two-way process. One example of this is processes associated with formally interviewing people as "veterans" of the problem about their knowledgeableness. This is work that David Epston has pioneered. And we can also employ people as consultants in a direct sense in regard to work that we actually do with people who seek our help, and in regard to the nature of our interaction with these people. This, of course, has a priority in regard to issues of culture, race, and so on, but can also be relevant with regard to age.

To this end, I have, on occasions, employed children as consultants in my work with other families with young children. This is a particularly important practice in situations where the issue of inequality in terms of power is particularly pressing.

Very often I meet with adolescents and their parents who are in conflict, and frequently I find that the adolescents feel quite outnumbered within the therapeutic context. Engaging another adolescent as a consultant in this work to represent an adolescent viewpoint, in a non-partisan way, so often does a great deal to actually undermine the polarisation that is so often experienced in these relationships between adolescents and their parents.

Chris: So, there are many accountability arrangements that you might enter into with the people who consult you.

Michael: Yes. But in placing an emphasis on such arrangements, I don't want to obscure the fact that accountability is a theme that plays itself out across the entire course of the therapy itself. For example, during my meetings with people, I consult them about how the conversation is going for them, about how they see its direction fitting or not fitting with the overall project, about how it is affecting them emotionally and otherwise, and so on. And at the beginning of all sessions subsequent to the first, I engage people in a review of the events that have taken place during the interval between sessions, and encourage them to review these against previous therapeutic conversations, so that we might determine the real effects of these conversations on their lives and their relationships. This makes it possible for the work to be evaluated, and renders the therapeutic interaction responsive to this evaluation. And, of course, this sort of consultation confronts therapists with the ethical responsibilities that they have in regard to the real effects of, or consequences of, their interactions with those people who seek their help.

Chris: I'm interested in your work with children, and the idea that I've often heard expressed, particularly within the area of education, that children don't have the sophistication to be able to fully participate in decision-making about policies that affect their lives. Can you imagine children themselves caucusing about, and participating in, this sort of accountability process?

Michael: Definitely. I think that the attitude that you are referring to reflects the ageism of our culture. And I think that these proposals for structures of accountability could possibly address this issue.

I know that it is possible to consult even very young children about their lives in ways that help them to articulate more clearly their own preferred purposes and goals, although, in our culture, this sort of consultation is far from routine. So often, when I meet with families that have young children, I find that very few of these children have actually been consulted about the problem that is of concern to others. As a result of this lack of consultation, children's knowledgeableness is not respected, and, as well, parents have taken a position on the problem, and other authorities have done the same, including those from schools, but the children themselves have not had the opportunity to do so.

These children can be successfully consulted about how they see problems affecting their lives and their relationships, and about whether or not they think that these effects are favourable. They can even be asked the sort of "why" questions that make it possible for them to justify these evaluations. When children have the opportunity to justify such evaluations, they wind up talking about their own preferred notions of purpose, of the wants that they have for their life, about their accounts of their own goals, and so on. Usually, these can be honoured by other family members, and invariably this leads to constructive action.

And I believe that this generation of, and articulation of, purposes, wants, goals, and so on, with reference to children's decision-making about policies in education, could be more effectively achieved through the sort of caucusing that is proposed by The Family Centre.

REFERENCES

Jenkins, A. 1990:
Invitations to Responsibility: The therapeutic engagement of men who are violent and abusive. Adelaide: Dulwich Centre Publications.
Tamasese, K. & Waldegrave, C. 1993:
"Cultural and gender accountability in the 'Just Therapy' approach." Journal of Feminist Family Therapy, 5(2):29-45. (Republished 1994 in Dulwich Centre Newsletter, Nos.2&3.)
White, M. 1991:
"Deconstruction & therapy." Dulwich Centre Newsletter, No.3.

7.   Reflecting Teamwork as Definitional Ceremony

The tradition of working with therapeutic teams, and the use of one-way screens in this work, is one that is well established in the field of family therapy. Many of the early developments in this sort of teamwork were pioneered by the Milan Associates, and by the faculty of the Ackerman Institute of New York. According to this tradition, the members of the team remained behind the one-way screen and were ever invisible to the people who were consulting them. It was the team's role to develop systems hypotheses - about the "family system" and about the "therapeutic system" - and to plan interventions, based on these hypotheses, to be delivered by the interviewer. Whatever the merits of this way of structuring team participation, and whatever the subsequent developments in theorising this work and in team focus, the autonomy and anonymity of the team raised various issues of an ethical and political nature that a number of therapists - including many of those who had played a significant role in the evolution of this tradition - began to confront.

In 1987 Tom Andersen of Norway published his paper *The Reflecting Team: Dialogue and meta-dialogue in clinical work*. This introduced the family therapy world to a very different conception of therapeutic teamwork, and to a very different notion of team member participation. These developments were enthusiastically embraced by many therapists who appreciated the possibilities associated with working with therapeutic teams, but who had found the ethical issues raised by the autonomous and anonymous team increasingly difficult to ignore.

Karl Tomm was one of these therapists, and he introduced me to the notion of the reflecting team in the late 1980s. Karl, ever alert to new possibilities in this work, and becoming increasingly concerned about ethical issues in the field, had arranged to meet with Tom Andersen to get some first-hand exposure to "reflecting team" work. He had come away from this meeting greatly enthused, and encouraged me to explore reflecting team structures in my own work. In response, I expressed some concerns - at least I half expressed some concerns, because I don't think that I quite knew how to put them very adequately in the first place - and raised some questions. I later managed to get my thoughts more organised around some of these concerns and questions, and they came out like this:

1. I had no difficulty in appreciating the fact that the reflecting team format could be a very powerful experience for people consulting therapists, but powerful in what sense? I had witnessed first-hand, on many occasions, the powerfully negative effect that the openness of the traditional ward-round can have on "patients" in psychiatric hospitals. So I was sure that there wasn't anything intrinsic to the openness of the reflecting team format that would necessarily render it therapeutic in its effects. What form might reflections take, I wondered, in order to mitigate the possible negative effects of this openness?

2. I was acutely aware of the fact that, in the culture of psychotherapy, most of the interactions between therapists and people who consult them are informed by the discourses of pathology. These discourses inform taken-for-granted ways of speaking about people's lives and relationship practices that have the effect of marginalising and objectifying people who seek help. What sort of requirements on reflecting team practices would be necessary to undermine this potential for marginalisation and objectification?

3. More specifically, I was familiar with the penchant of many family

therapists to engage in the time-honoured structuralist and functionalist analyses of the events of people's lives. Among other things, these analyses and the operations associated with them have the effect of elevating expert knowledge claims to "truth" status, and of disqualifying the knowledges of persons who consult therapists. So I could see a potential for the reflecting team context to be one that was maximising of both the imposition of the "truth" claims of the professional knowledges and the disqualification of alternative claims. What guidelines might be established for reflecting teamwork that could provide for some check on this, guidelines that might minimise the possibilities for this disqualification, that might limit the possibilities for imposition?

4.   I had a degree of awareness of the extent to which the culture of psychotherapy is not peripheral to mainstream culture - of the extent to which it is not exempt from dominant structures and ideologies, and of the extent to which it plays a central role in the reproduction of these structures and ideologies (for example, just take the link between the misogyny of dominant culture and the mother-blaming of the culture of psychotherapy). In the light of this, could we trust that the reflecting team, in its operations, would not also be complicit in this reproduction, and that it would not unwittingly contribute further to the very forces that provide the context for the problems that people seek consultation over? Certainly such trust would be misplaced. So, what reflecting team processes might be instated to address this vulnerability to the reproduction of some of the negative aspects of dominant culture?

Over several years, I have received various responses to my expressions of these and other concerns. Some therapists have suggested that I am making the whole idea of reflecting teamwork too complicated, and that I should learn to trust the "intuitiveness" of team members. But I could not be convinced of this. To be intuitive is to enter into a discourse of understanding and practice that is considerably informed by what might be called "folk psychology". This is not to suggest that intuition can't be positive in its effects on people's lives, but I don't believe that it should go unexamined. I have no doubt that a study of the history of intuition would be illuminating of a particular system of understanding and acting in the world - that we would find many discontinuities in what counts as intuition through time, and that we would be confronted by many examples of the extent to which yesterday's intuition so often seems like today's folly. To encourage team members to "trust" their intuition would be like encouraging one to simply have faith in their own good intentions, which often isn't a very good idea at all.

Other therapists suggested that I could resolve my concerns by simply leaving it to team members to express the subjective experience that emanates from the "centre" of their being. What about this notion of unexamined expression of experience? Is there such thing as a pure expression of subjective experience? Can any expression of experience avoid the mediating effects of systems of understanding? Can any expression of experience in language stand outside of what it is that language constructs? Can any expression of one's experience within a community of persons be recognised by others standing outside of a system of meaning that provides for the response that we call recognition? Not likely! Besides, the whole idea of people having a centre through which they can express their essential self does not stand up at all well to close analysis.

Yet other therapists suggested that notions like Habermas' "ideal speech community" might relieve me of some of the burden of these concerns. But this didn't work at all well for me. I had some familiarity with this notion, but could not see how any community could possibly be exempt from the various relations of power of our culture and its institutions, including those based on gender, race, class, opportunity, age, sexual preference, economics, and so on. I had long held the view that it is through the recognition of these relations of power, not through a denial of them, that action can be taken to challenge them and reduce their toxicity, and that any such actions themselves play a part in relations of power. Because of this, I was more attracted to Foucault's critique of the notion of an ideal speech community than I was to the original proposal:

The thought that there could be a state of communication which would be such that the games of truth could circulate freely, without obstacles, without constraint and without coercive effects, seems to me to be Utopia. It is being blind to the fact that relations of power are not something bad in themselves, from which one must free one's self. I don't believe there can be a society without relations of power, if you understand them as means by which individuals try to conduct, to determine the behaviour of others. The problem is not of trying to dissolve them in the utopia of a perfectly transparent communication, but to give one's self the rules of law, the techniques of management, and also the ethics, the ethos, the practice of self, which would allow these games of power to be played with a minimum of domination. (Foucault 1988, p.18)

The questions and the concerns that I had were stubborn (and they still are, they just won't go away). But I continued to wrestle with them, because I remained enthusiastic about the transformative potential of reflecting teamwork, and because my early explorations of this format were mostly reinforcing. In this paper, I will describe a reflecting team structure that has evolved (a) through further explorations of these concerns, (b) in response to the comments of the many therapists who have stepped into reflecting teamwork at Dulwich Centre, and (c) from the feedback I have received about this work from people who have consulted me within these contexts.

During this discussion, I will not be referring to other conceptions and developments of reflecting teamwork because of a lack of familiarity with these. I have no doubt that other therapists have also been addressing concerns and questions similar to those I have outlined above, but I've not had the opportunity to catch up with their proposals and their translations of these into practice. And I don't know how Tom Andersen has responded to such concerns and questions, as it has not so far been possible for me to consult him about this, and I do not have a first-hand account of his work.

Now for a cautionary note. In the work that I will be describing here, I am not at all certain that I have yet satisfactorily addressed the sort of concerns and questions that I have outlined above, and I also acknowledge that there are many other concerns and questions that can be raised. So I would appreciate it if readers were to read this paper as an account of work in progress.

DEFINITIONAL CEREMONIES

Sometimes conditions conspire to make a generational cohort acutely self-conscious and then they become active participants in their own history and provide their own sharp, insistent definitions of themselves and explanations for their destiny, past and future. They are then knowing actors in a historical drama they script, rather than subjects of someone else's study. They "make" themselves, sometimes even "make themselves up," an activity which is not inevitable or automatic but reserved for special people in special circumstances. (Myerhoff 1982, p.100)

There exist many candidate metaphors for the sort of reflecting teamwork that I will be introducing in this discussion. To the extent that the reflecting teamwork that I am describing here establishes "conditions that conspire" to engage people as "active participants in their own history" and in "making themselves up", I believe that Barbara Myerhoff's "definitional ceremony" provides a particularly appropriate metaphor for this work, and serves to clarify some of the processes involved in it.

Myerhoff used this metaphor to describe some of the activities of an elderly, poor, and neglected Jewish community in Venice, Los Angeles. Because the people of this community were relatively invisible to the wider community, they were deprived of important reflections on their own lives, and at risk of becoming invisible to themselves - at risk of doubting their very existence. It was by "definitional ceremonies" that the people of this community countered this threat. These ceremonies provided for these people an "arena for appearing" and for "opportunities for self - and collective proclamations of being":

> *Definitional ceremonies deal with the problems of invisibility and marginality; they are strategies that provide opportunities for being seen and in one's own terms, garnering witnesses to one's worth, vitality and being.* (Myerhoff 1986, p.267)

Myerhoff calls attention to the critical role that the "outsider-witness" plays in these definitional ceremonies. These outsider witnesses are essential to the processes of the acknowledgement and the authentication of people's claims about their histories and about their identities, and to the performance of these claims. The participation of the outsider-witnesses in definitional ceremonies gives "greater public and factual" character to these claims, serving to amplify them and to authorise them. The outsider-witness also contributes to a context for reflexive self-consciousness - in which people become more conscious of themselves as they see themselves, and more conscious of their participation in the production of their productions of their lives. The achievement of this reflexive self-consciousness is not insignificant - it establishes a knowing that "knowing is a component of their conduct", making it possible for people to "assume responsibility for inventing themselves and yet maintain their sense of authenticity and integrity", for people to become aware of options for intervening in the shaping of their lives.

I believe that the ideas and the practices associated with the sort of reflecting teamwork that I will be describing in this paper introduce similar possibilities for the establishment of a reflexive self-consciousness and for participation in the authoring of one's own life. And I also believe that an understanding of the mechanisms of transformation in definitional ceremonies can serve to inform therapists of some of the more critical components of this work. This is certainly the case in the development of an understanding of the significance of team members as "outsider witnesses" in pushing forward the plot.

These old Jews . . . (in) . . . separating the curtains between the
real and unreal, imagined and actual, to step across the threshold
and draw with them, pulling behind them, witnesses who find,
often to their surprise, that they are somehow participating in
someone else's drama. . . . Having stepped over threshold, they
become the "fifth business", witnesses who push a plot forward
almost unwittingly; their story is not wholly their own but lives on,
woven into the stuff of other people's lives. (Myerhoff 1986,
p.284)

GENERAL ORIENTATION

My experience of reflecting teamwork is limited to training contexts
at Dulwich Centre and at workshops elsewhere. For many of the therapists
attending these programs, this will be their first introduction to the notion
of the reflecting team, and to reflecting team practices. Because of this, I
find that it is helpful, at the outset, to provide them with a general
orientation.

As part of this orientation, I tell visiting therapists that they will be
discouraged from theorising about the "truth" of the problems that people
bring to therapy. Instead, it will be their task to attend carefully to the
discussion that is taking place during the interview. I also inform them that
I will be discouraging them from the idea that it is their role to prepare
and to deliver some intervention into people's lives or into the "system". It
is not the task of team members to "strategise", to "problem-solve", to
"teach", to "role-model", to "perturb", or to advise.

Therapists are informed that engaging in the activities that are
associated with this theorising and with the preparation of interventions will
subtract from a consciousness of the privileged nature of their position in
three senses of this:

1. The privilege that is granted to team members by those people who
    open their lives to others in the course of this work - an act of

inclusion that reflects an extraordinary act of faith and of trust in the therapeutic team.

2. The privilege that relates to the personal location of team members in terms of the social order - in responding to the events of their own lives, team members so often have options for action and lifestyle choices that people who consult them more often than not do not have.

3. The privilege, in terms of power, that team members enjoy within the therapeutic context - there is an inherent imbalance of power in therapeutic contexts that favours therapists and team members, regardless of the various measures that might be taken to render these contexts more egalitarian.

Also, as part of this orientation, it is my habit to provide visiting therapists with some general guidelines about the nature of the responses that are expected of the reflecting team. It will be their task to interact with each other and with those people who are seeking consultation in ways that are:

1. Informed by a degree of consciousness of the privileged nature of their position in the context of this work.

2. Acknowledging of people's experiences of the problems over which they are seeking consultation, of the dilemmas that they have faced, and of the struggles that they have engaged in over their efforts to change what they have wanted to change in their lives.

3. Provoking of people's fascination with certain of the more neglected aspects of their lives, aspects that might provide a point of entry for the generation and/or resurrection of the alternative stories of their lives.

4.   Situating of their own responses within the context of their own personal experience, imagination, purposes, curiosity, and so on.

STRUCTURE OF THE MEETING

When I am working with reflecting teams, I usually propose that the meeting be structured in four parts, with each part constituting an interview in itself. In the first part, the interviewer meets with the people who are seeking consultation, while the team members take their position as an audience to this conversation. At this time, team members can be behind a one-way screen, viewing the session on closed circuit television, or can be in the interviewing room but sitting back from the interviewer and the people who are seeking consultation. At the outset of the interview, people are given the option of meeting the team members before getting started, or of meeting them as they introduce themselves prior to commencing their reflections in the second part of the interview. As well, people have the option of taking away with them a list of the names of team members, and details of their workplaces.

In the second part, the interviewer and the people seeking consultation switch places with the team - they now become the audience to the conversation that takes place amongst the team members. During this time, team members reflect on, and actively interview each other about, their experiences of the first part of the meeting - that is, in the first interview. This constitutes the second interview. On occasion, some have experienced difficulty entering into interactions with each other in this way, and have tended to direct their reflections to the interviewer and to the people who are now in the audience role - the idea of having a conversation with team members about the lives of others while in their presence breaks most of the rules about therapeutic encounters. However, these team members soon become more relaxed with, and enthusiastic about, these third-party conversations once they have had the opportunity to hear from people first-hand about the beneficial effects of the opportunity of witnessing one's life being spoken about so respectfully in one's presence.

In the third part of the meeting, everybody switches place again, and the interviewer interviews the people seeking consultation about their experiences of the first interview and the second interview, with the team again taking up the audience position. This constitutes the third interview.

In the fourth part of the meeting, the interviewer, the team members, and the people seeking consultation get together to debrief and to engage in a deconstruction of the therapy itself. This constitutes the fourth interview.

I will here provide some details about the particularities of the second, third and fourth interviews. In doing so, I intend to assume some familiarity with the general therapeutic practices that I refer to. I have discussed these practices in some detail in various publications, and would prefer not to reiterate them in this paper.

Second Interview: Four Classes of Response

1. **Joining**

Team members introduce themselves, explain their presence at the consultation, and provide brief details to locate themselves in the field (e.g. workplace, projects, interests etc.) so that they do not remain anonymous to the people who are seeking the consultation. Rather than doing this by way of a round, it is usually more helpful for team members to make this introduction just before engaging in their first response. This way, people are not overwhelmed by details about the identities of reflecting team members, but are able to link these identities to the interests of these team members as they introduce themselves across the course of the meeting.

Team members ensure that all of the persons seeking consultation are acknowledged. This can be achieved, in part, by one or two members of the team providing some account of their understanding of (i) the circumstances that have led people to seek the consultation, and (ii) these people's experiences of these circumstances. Apart from experiencing acknowledgement at this time, the people seeking consultation develop an understanding of the understandings that team members have about their predicaments, and about this they can give feedback to the team members at a later stage in the meeting.

2. Mystery

Team members respond to those developments that have been judged by the people, during the first interview, to be preferred developments - that is, those sparkling moments, exceptions, unique outcomes, or contradictions that were identified during the first part of the meeting. Alternatively, team members can respond to those developments that they believe *might* constitute preferred developments to the people seeking consultation - but, in this case, care is taken to acknowledge the fact that this response remains in the realm of speculation until confirmed or refuted by the people concerned.

Team members respond to these preferred developments as one might respond to a mystery - one that an outsider can be curious about, but one that only those people with the inside knowledge can satisfactorily unravel. In making this response, team members convey their faith in the ability of people to unravel these mysteries of their lives, even if this cannot be achieved instantaneously and independently, but over time in collaborative projects with interested parties. These preferred developments provide points of entry to the alternative stories of people's lives.

Orienting to mystery in this way is generative of the curiosity of team members, and, in turn, this curiosity is provocative of a fascination in people for some of the previously neglected but significant experiences of their lives.

3. Alternative Landscapes

Those preferred developments that are generative of the curiosity of team members can be considered points of entry or gateways to the alternative stories of people's lives. These alternative stories provide access to alternative knowledges about ways of being and thinking in the world. To assist people to step through these gateways, so that they might explore some of the possibilities that are before them for the re-authoring of their lives, at this stage in the second interview team members traffic in "landscape of action" and "landscape of consciousness" questions. As I have provided considerable information about the development of these questions in various publications, I do not intend to provide an overview of this here. However, I will provide some examples of landscape of action and landscape of consciousness questions taken from reflecting team interactions so that readers might have some sense of how these go in this context:

Team Member A *I found that my attention was very much captured by the steps that Simon initiated here to challenge some of the old habits that have been quite dominant. Was this interesting to anyone else here? - because I would really like to talk about this some.*

Team Member B *I also had a sense that these were important steps. It left me wondering about how Simon had prepared the way for these steps, because I'm sure that they didn't just come out of the blue. Did anyone here notice anything that would give some clue about this?*

Team Member C *Perhaps. Early in the discussion, I heard Anne say something about Simon doing a bit more exercising. Perhaps this was something that he was doing to get ready for these steps.*

Team Member D *Yes, I was interested in the fact that Anne brought*

this to our attention here today. *This*
acknowledgement seemed important to Simon, and
this gave me some sense of what Anne's
contribution to these developments might be.

Team Member B *What do you think these developments reflect about*
what Simon wants for his life, and what do you
think they say about this mother/son relationship?

Team Member A *Perhaps that Simon is interested in having options*
for his life, perhaps that he wants to be able to take
good care of his life, perhaps that he has some idea
about having a bit more to say about how his life
goes.

Team Member B *And what about the qualities in the mother/son*
relationship?

Team Member D *This is a good question. Simon and Anne are*
listening to our conversation, and I wonder what
their answer to this question might be? My guess is
that they could tell some interesting stories about the
history of their relationship that would illustrate
these qualities.

Team Member C *I've had some thoughts about what these qualities*
might be.

In this example, team members first interact with each other
around landscape of action questions, then reference landscape of
consciousness questions to their speculation in the landscape of
action, then reference landscape of action questions to their
speculation in the landscape of consciousness, and later go on from
here in the zig-zagging fashion that I have described elsewhere. All
of this is for the purposes of opening options for Anne and Simon
to thicken and more deeply root some of the counterplots of their
lives.

Throughout this second interview, the people sitting behind the
one-way screen become more fascinated by some of the alternative

landscapes of their own lives. They speculate about the answers to these questions and, in the process, achieve some clarity in their own thoughts about the different connections between some of the neglected events of their lives, and about the counterplots that these connections suggest.

As readers will note, the reflecting team process is one in which team members actively interview each other - it is not a process that can be described as "pointing out positives". This work is not based on the tradition of behaviourism - it is not founded on the notion of positive reinforcement.

Reflecting teamwork based on the notion of positive reinforcement can so easily degenerate into a barrage of disconnected comments which can be confusing and disorientating for people. As well, under these circumstances, reflecting team members can be experienced as patronising and out of touch with the realities of people's lives. Further, it is not at all difficult for people to think that team members are ingenuine, just trying to be positive in order to "jolly them along". And as well as all of these hazards, team members usually find it tedious to be operating in this way. In their reflections they frequently find themselves "reinventing the wheel", and that their conversations are reduced to a level of banality, in which one superlative is exchanged for another. Although I caricature this sort of reflecting team conversation here, I have been informed that at times they come perilously and embarrassingly close to this in actuality:

Team Member E *I was really impressed by this development.*

Team Member F *Yes, me too. But don't you think that this other development was simply stunning?*

Team Member G *Look, I know that these developments were really good, but there was this other event that was clearly exceptional.*

Team Member H *Yes, I agree, and would like to offer my congratulations on this. But I must tell you that I*

> *was really blown away by the news of what*
> *happened when they got together on this. Blown*
> *away, I tell you.*

Team Member I   *Wow, me too. Umm, ummm* . . . [searching for
other superlative, and thinking about trying "over
the moon" or maybe "volcanic"].

When reflecting team members have the opportunity to actually
interview each other about their comments and their questions, and
are oriented in this by the narrative metaphor, then the outcome
cannot be some disconnected series of superlatives, or a barrage of
unrelated comments and questions - the work becomes thematic.

Very often therapists find the notion of reflecting team
members interviewing each other a relatively new notion, and they
can have difficulty in maintaining this during the course of the team
response. This difficulty can be addressed by suggesting that one team
member undertake to monitor the discussion, and, if necessary,
provide a prompt from time to time: "Look, I think that we are going
off the track here. This work is meant to be structured along the line
of a series of interviews."

Throughout the reflecting team interaction, team members are
careful to avoid the indicative, and instead frame their responses to
each other in the subjunctive mood of "as if", "maybe", "possibly", and
so on. In this way, team members can avoid participating in the
construction of settled certainties.

4.   Deconstruction

There is always an unequal distribution of power in the
therapeutic context, regardless of the steps that are taken by
therapists to render the context of therapy more egalitarian. And as
previously discussed, the potential for this unequal distribution of
power to be disqualifying and objectifying of people is greater in team
contexts. In view of this, it is important that steps be taken to counter

possible toxic effects of this power imbalance, to reduce the potential for harm. One contribution to such steps is for reflecting team members to assist each other to deconstruct their responses. This can be achieved if team members invite each other to embody their comments with, or to situate their speech acts in, the history of their personal experience, interests, intentions, imagination, and so on. If reflecting team members take responsibility to deconstruct their comments and questions in this way, this does provide at least some safeguard against the sort of impositions of "truth" that are the outcome of disembodied speech acts.

This deconstruction of the comments and questions of team members occurs more towards the end of the reflecting team response. It is not usually necessary for all of the team's responses to be deconstructed, because when people experience a few instances of this, they begin to take all team members comments as situated and authoritative in terms of personal experience, but not in terms of claims to some privileged access to objective knowledge. Sometimes it is wise for team members to select for deconstruction those questions and comments that seemed most emphatic, or those that might have had the greatest potential to be read as advice or judgement.

Example 1

Team Member J   *I've found this discussion really interesting, and I remember that we got into it following a question that you asked about how this couple had managed to arrive at this point. What got you curious about this in the first place?*

Team Member K   *As I said, I knew that it wasn't very far back that this couple were at what we might call point A. Now it appeared to me that, although they hadn't achieved what they wanted to achieve, they weren't still at point A, but somewhere down the track,* maybe at point D. So, I wanted to know the B and the C of it.

Team Member J   *Yes, but what was your intention in drawing this out with Donna and John listening to this? What effect did you think that your comments would have on them?*

Team Member K   *I was thinking that when people take steps that are not all that visible to them, it is hard for them to take a leaf out of their own book with regard to future steps. So I figured that if these steps were more visible to John and Donna, they could look back at them, and that this would give them more of a sense of the path that they are on, and that this would help them to know more about where to place their next steps.*

Example 2

Team Member L   *I'd like to go back a way to ask you about why you assumed that this development was so important?*

Team Member M   *It seemed so obvious to me, and it sure seemed significant to the rest of the team.*

Team Member L   *Yes I agree that it did. But of all the people in the team, why were you the first to pick up on this? Was this something to do with your personal experiences of life, or something else?*

Team Member M   *I don't know if I actually thought about this. But, as we are talking, I am aware of the fact that, when I was Sue's age, I was going through some of the same things that she is going through with her parents. And somehow we all got through it, but I never really figured out how - at least not completely. I was aware of my mother's contribution to resolving things, but now I am thinking that my father may have played some part in working this out as well. So I am going away with some questions to ask him that I didn't have before this interview.*

Example 3

Team Member N *You have responded quite enthusiastically to the efforts that Alexandria has been putting into her relationship with her daughter. I would like to know where you were coming from in your comments.*

Team Member O *Your question has caught me off guard. I'd like to reflect on it some, so could I pass on this for the time being, and perhaps come back to it closer to the end of our discussion after I've had more time to think on it?*

Team Member N *Okay. That's fine.*

Team Member N (sometime later) *We have nearly run out of time, and I've been wondering whether you've had any thoughts about that question?*

Team Member O *You know, I have. When my daughter was the same age as Christine, many years ago, I had the same concerns about her that Alexandria has about Christine. And I felt quite inadequate in my attempts to address these concerns, and have always felt that I let her down somewhat. But getting in touch with all of the efforts that Alexandria has put into getting this right, and the fact that she is also a sole parent, has helped me to appreciate what I was up against in getting things right, and all of the effort that went into this. So this interview has been very important to me for many reasons.*

When team members take some responsibility to deconstruct

their comments and questions in this way, this has the effect of countering the objectification and the marginalisation of those people who seek therapy. As well, the transparency that is the outcome of this is authenticating of the team members contributions - their interest and their curiosity are not experienced by people as academic. Also, as this embodiment of the responses of the reflecting team members counters the possibility that their "truths" might be imposed on people's lives, it provides for a more egalitarian therapeutic context.

In regard to the practice of situating one's comments and curiosity within the context of one's personal experience, team members take care not to engage in the expression of their experience for the sake of the expression of their experience, and, in so doing, also take care not to provide a "moral story" or "homily" (which is unlikely to happen if team members have entered the conversation through the route of curiosity).

This sharing of personal experience is not "indulgent" in its form. It is clearly not in the tradition of the "bare-it-all" approaches; it is not about team members expressing all of their distressing and difficult experiences with people who seek consultation. This sharing of personal experience is not done with the goal of smuggling in "Here, take a leaf out of my book". It is not undertaken to give people the sense that the team member concerned has arrived somewhere in life. And it is not gratuitous. But this sharing of experience is purposeful, and undertaken in cognisance of, and in a way that it is honouring of, the therapeutic contract.

Team members do not meet together before the second interview to prepare their comments and questions. And as their interaction evolves across the second interview, they often find themselves talking about what they would not have imagined they would be talking about ahead of their reflections. At times, team members find themselves contemplating previously forgotten or half-forgotten memories, and filling gaps in the primary narrative of their own lives. At times, team members find themselves talking about or thinking about their own lives in different ways, ways that contribute to an entirely new appreciation of some of the events of their lives. And, at times, team members have vivid experiences of some of the alternative stories of their lives, ones that bring new options for action. Whatever the case, this reflecting teamwork is shaping of the lives of team members. They emerge from this work with their lives remade. In various ways, they have become other than who they were before their participation in the reflecting team. Needless to say, team members are unlikely to find this work tedious, but invigorating.

Third Interview

In the third part of the meeting, everybody switches place again, as the people who sought the consultation are interviewed about their responses to it, with the team members taking their place as an audience to this conversation. This interview first focuses on people's experiences of the second interview - that is, the reflecting team discussion - and then on their experiences of the first interview. At this time, the interviewer also shares his/her responses to the reflecting team's comments, his/her thoughts about what s/he would be interested in taking up at the next meeting, and solicits the people's responses to this.

People can be asked to give feedback about those comments and questions which particularly caught their attention, or which seemed helpful, and to distinguish these from those that didn't seem relevant or that were unhelpful. They can then be interviewed about those comments and questions that were significant to them, on the understanding that the interviewer and the team members can't know in advance what will be most helpful in this work, and that what is learned from this interview will be relied upon to guide the work itself.

This is also the time at which the interviewer can ask future-oriented questions that open up space for the exploration of possibilities for action. For example, the feedback that the interviewer receives at this point may suggest that one of the reflecting team comments was particularly significant in that it brought with it an important realisation. In response to this, people can be interviewed about what they predict to be the effects of this realisation. How might this shape their responses to the sort of events for which they sought consultation? What might help them to keep this realisation close at hand over the forthcoming weeks?

Fourth Interview

In the fourth part of the meeting, everybody gets together - the interviewer, the people who sought the consultation, and the team members. At this time, it is the process of the interview itself, and its deconstruction, that is the focus of discussion. Usually (although not necessarily), at the outset of the fourth interview, the interviewer is interviewed by team members about the specifics of his/her participation - for example, about why s/he asked certain questions and not other questions, about what these questions were in response to, about other questions that s/he might have liked to have asked, about what s/he was thinking about at particular points during the meeting and about how this informed his/her comments at this time, about what his/her intentions were in regard to certain responses over the course of the interview, about the sort of personal experiences that might have been influential in determining these responses, and so on.

The interviewer can then reciprocate by interviewing team members about their thoughts on some of the possibilities that might have been more fully explored during the meeting, the line of questioning that they believe may have assisted this exploration, their proposals for following up what they believe important to follow up at the next interview, their predictions about the possible outcome of doing so, and so on. At this time, the interviewer can also interview team members about some of their team reflections.

As this fourth interview develops, team members are free to interview other team members about these matters, and the people who have sought the consultation are also invited to join in this. Because of the prevailing cultural construction of therapy, and because of the power differential implicit in this work, it is initially difficult for people to accept these invitations to join with the interviewer and the team in this way, but after one or two experiences they become more active in the formulation of questions.

There is the option for the interviewer and team members to invite those people who sought the consultation to comment on their experience of specific comments, questions, and any other events that occurred at any time during the three interviews. And, as well, team members can solicit people's feedback about the structure of the work itself. It is important that the therapist and the team members avoid loaded questions that are in any way judging of each other's contribution. And it is important that this fourth interview not just become an interview of family members, because, should this eventuate, the opportunity for deconstruction of the therapy itself would be lost.

The interviewing that constitutes the fourth part of the meeting provides, among other things, an opportunity for those people seeking consultation to "come behind the scenes and join in on the ground floor" so that they might have access to the workings of the therapy. To achieve this, the interaction between the therapist and team members is structured according to the principle of transparency (see White 1991), and care must be taken to draw an adequate distinction between interaction around this principle, and around those principles which shape many of the team's responses in the second interview. Being true to this principle will not be possible if team members use the fourth part of the meeting for the purposes of further reflections of a re-authoring nature. To achieve a participation that is guided by this principle of transparency requires a reorientation, and at times team members find that this poses a difficult transition to navigate. Because of this, it is sometimes desirable to assign to one team member the role of monitoring the discussion, so that they might, when necessary, call the attention of other team members to the priorities at hand.

At the end of this fourth interview, the people who sought the consultation are invited to have the last say - to inform interviewer and team members of those ideas which were of most interest, to give an indication of those lines of questioning that they believe hold the most promise, and to provide feedback about any speculation on the possibilities that might be taken up at the next session.

The feedback that people give about this fourth interview is invariably positive - they respond to this transparency with enthusiasm - and many find this to be very significantly "therapeutic". These findings contradict an idea that is at large within the culture of psychotherapy - that if people know what we are up to in this work, then it won't have its desired effect. In the case of the ideas and practices that I have been referring to in this paper, it is apparent that the more transparent we are about what we are up to, the more helpful it is to those who are seeking consultation.

EVALUATION

Quite some time ago, I undertook an informal evaluation of the sort of reflecting teamwork that is informed by the ideas and the structures outlined in this paper. This was undertaken on a basis similar to that of David Epston's study of the value of therapeutic documents which is reported on elsewhere in this collection - "How many sessions worth of good therapy is a good reflecting team discussion?" The outcome of this evaluation was fascinating - at an average of 4.7 sessions of good therapy, it was very close to David's figure of 4.5 for therapeutic documents. Since this informal evaluation, there have been a number of significant developments in this reflecting teamwork, and I have a plan to undertake a more formal re-evaluation of this work in the near future.

My informal evaluation of this work was of the more structured approach to reflecting teamwork, in which, during the first three stages, the team members and the people seeking consultation were audiences to each other's conversations, but not engaged directly in discussion with each other. I have explored other arrangements in this work, including unstructured discussions between the people seeking consultation and reflecting team members. When people have experienced both arrangements, their preference is invariably for the more structured approach. Upon enquiring about the basis of this preference, I received responses like:

- *If you get into a discussion with the team, this has the effect of depriving you of the option of standing outside of your life and experiencing it from a different perspective.*
- *I found it more helpful to sit back from my life, and to be an audience to the team, rather than sitting in my life in direct discussion with the team.*
- *When I interacted with the team in the second part, I didn't experience the same thing. It wasn't as powerful, and I think that this was because I was so busy editing what people said, and at times censoring what they said.*
- *When it was my turn to listen to the team, I felt that I was somewhere else, not with the problem. I could see how I didn't have to be with the problem. This didn't happen the time when I was talking with the team. It's not that I didn't enjoy talking with the team, but it just wasn't the same as listening to them.*
- *There is something that is so much more powerful about listening to a conversation about your life that is acknowledging and respectful of who you are.*

CONCLUSION

I have discussed reflecting team practices that are isomorphic with the practices of what has come to be known as *narrative therapy*. I have no first-hand familiarity with other forms of reflecting teamwork, and so I am not in a position to compare and contrast the work that I have described here with other approaches. The reflecting team practices that I have detailed here provide people with a deep sense of acknowledgement and with opportunities to break with many aspects of their life as they know it. As well, it has become clear that teamwork of this sort provides for people something akin to a quantum leap in possibilities for the re-authoring of their lives, and in options for action in the world.

I believe that the ideas and practices of this work go some way towards (a) providing a check on the potential for the power imbalance, which is inherent in such contexts, to do harm, (b) assisting therapists to break from the discourses of pathology and from formal systems of analysis that are so marginalising and objectifying of people - in fact, I believe that these ideas and practices can play a part in undoing the effects of these experiences, (c) challenging the supremacy of expert knowledges, (d) privileging alternative knowledge systems, (e) providing some options to address the propensity of therapeutic contexts to reproduce many of the negative aspects of the structures and ideologies of the dominant culture. However, I am not satisfied that those developments in the reflecting teamwork that I have described here go far enough in all of this, and this provides me with the impetus to engage in further explorations of this work.

This account of reflecting teamwork does not exhaust the possibilities at any level. For example, to facilitate the deconstruction of the therapy itself in the fourth interview, the interviewer, the team members and the people who sought the consultation can sit down together and undertake a microanalysis of the selected videotaped segments of the first three interviews. Non-therapists can be prepared for participation in reflecting teamwork - that is, family members, other relatives, friends and acquaintances, peers, etc. - and there are many contexts in which this work might be introduced - in schools, in workplaces, at the special meetings of various communities, and so on. And there are options for creating reflecting team contexts when working solo or in isolation.

Here, at the conclusion of this paper, I would like to acknowledge my debt to Tom Andersen for originating reflecting teamwork. It was his conception of this work that stimulated my own explorations of it. To the reader, I wish you all well in your own explorations of reflecting teamwork. Perhaps someday we will cross paths and have the opportunity to swap notes on this.

REFERENCES

Andersen, T. 1987:
"The reflecting team: Dialogue and meta-dialogue in clinical work."
Family Process, 26:415-428.

Foucault, M. 1988:
"The ethic of care for the self as a practice of freedom." In
Bernauer, J. & Rasmussen, D. (Eds), **The Final Foucault**.
Cambridge: MIT Press.

Myerhoff, B. 1982:
"Life history among the elderly: Performance, visibility and
remembering." In Ruby, J. (Ed), **A Crack in The Mirror. Reflexive
perspectives in anthropology.** Philadelphia: University of
Pennsylvania Press.

Myerhoff, B. 1986:
"Life not death in Venice: Its second life." In Turner, V. & Bruner,
E. (Eds), **The Anthropology of Experience**. Chicago: University of
Illinois Press.

White, M. 1991:
"Deconstruction and therapy." **Dulwich Centre Newsletter**, No.3.

8.   Therapeutic Documents Revisited

Since the publication of *Narrative means to therapeutic ends*, David Epston and I have persisted with our exploration of different forms of therapeutic documents in our work with those people who consult us, and have continued to find these explorations highly reinforcing of this practice. Because of this, it is my sense that this collection would hardly be complete without some further discussion of therapeutic documents.

Although most of the therapists we meet can appreciate the merits of writing to the people who consult them, they often ask us questions about the extent to which we think that the time and energy spent on the preparation of such documents is warranted, particularly in circumstances where there is a high demand for therapeutic services and a scarcity of resources available to meet this demand. "Can the outlay of time and energy that goes into the preparation of these therapeutic documents be justified?" is a question that we so often hear, particularly from administrators and co-ordinators of counselling and social service agencies.

In response to questions of this sort, some time ago David engaged in some informal research into the value of therapeutic documents. He arranged to meet with a number of people who had consulted him, and invited them to assess the value of the documents that they had put together in their work with him. These people asked what measure they might use in determining the value of these documents, and to this David replied: "Well, was the receipt of a letter as valuable to you as a whole session of therapy, or half a session of therapy, or did it subtract from your experience of the therapy?" In response to this question, those people who were connoisseurs of therapy asked, "Do you mean what was this letter worth in terms of poor therapy, mediocre therapy, or good therapy?" "Good therapy, good therapy", exclaimed David. Initially people's responses to this question surprised David. Some people said seven sessions, some said ten, some said three, and some said one. David did a quick calculation, and came up with an average of 4.5! So, it has now been established, that a good therapeutic document is worth 4.5 sessions of good therapy. David undertook this evaluation some time ago, and it is probably time that we conducted a more systematised and formal evaluation. If we do manage to find the time to undertake this, my guess is that we will find the figures that David came up with some years ago quite conservative.

So, in response to questions about whether the time and energy that goes into the preparation of such letters can be justified, our response would be, "How could a decision *not* to engage in this practice be justified?" After all, even if one of these documents took one hour of a therapist's time to prepare, then, considering that the average duration of an interview is one hour, by my calculations the therapist has saved three and a half hours of their own time, or three and a half hours of agency time!

However, settling this question opens a floodgate of other questions, and these stretch all the way from questions about introducing people to the idea of therapeutic letters through to questions about therapists' responses to people's responses to receiving these. Here, I intend to take up just two of these questions and will attempt to provide at least a partial answer to them:

1.   "What thoughts do you have for streamlining the process of letter writing so that it might be less time consuming?", and

2.   "Okay, so what do you when you have gone to the effort to put together a letter, and, having sent it off in the mail, later find out that it was received only to be put in the hallstand drawer along with the bills and not read by anyone?"

In response to the first question, I am going to introduce readers to what I call *simple translations* and *statements of position*. Simple translations and statements of position are not at all time consuming - in fact they require the investment of a bare minimum of "non-contact time" from therapists. And yet, such therapeutic documents are highly effective. I will present information about these types of documents through illustration. I have not chosen "exemplary" illustrations for this purpose, but ones that I consider "run-of-the-mill".

In response to the second question, I will take readers through a checklist which will certainly diminish the likelihood that therapists will experience the "hallstand drawer" phenomenon. I think that therapists who are just embarking on explorations of therapeutic documents will find this checklist particularly useful. Those therapists who are some way down the track in their explorations of therapeutic documents will probably find that they have more informally and generally incorporated many of the points of this checklist into their interviews.

SIMPLE TRANSLATIONS

Nicholas Harris,[1] aged 11 years, was brought to see me by his parents over their concerns about bed-wetting. This bed-wetting had resisted many, many attempts to resolve it, and it was becoming increasingly embarrassing for Nicholas, and, as well, more significantly constraining of his life. Not only did it make it impossible for him to sleep over with friends, but it was preventing him from stepping into many of the activities that were available to his peers - for example, going away on camp. It was also clear to me that this problem was now also having a demoralising effect on Nicholas's parents. They despaired of this problem ever being resolved.

I asked Nicholas what the bed-wetting was talking him into about the sort of person he was. Was it convincing him of positive things about who who he was as a person, or was it convincing him of negative things about

---

1. To preserve confidentiality, all names in this paper are fictitious.

who he was as a person? Questions of this sort introduce externalizing conversations that accomplish several objectives. They provide the opportunity for people to make public their private stories of identity, and to step into a position that is once removed from these stories. From this position people begin to experience a degree of alienation from these private stories of identity, and to break from the negative "truths" about who they are that are borne by these stories - negative "truths" that have been so capturing of them in the past.

In response to these questions, and with the assistance of his parents, I learned from Nicholas that the bed-wetting problem was talking him into the idea that he was "incompetent". Further questions established that, for Nicholas, not only did incompetence represent one of his negative "truths" of identity, but that, in a more general sense, it represented a "dominant plot" in his life, one that had been quite influential in shaping his life.

The naming of the dominant plot in this way introduces many possibilities for the identification of what I have variously referred to as *unique outcomes, contradictions, sparkling events,* and so on. According to my definition, a unique outcome is a contradiction to the dominant plot, and might be a contradiction to the problem, but this is by no means always the case. To conceive of the unique outcome as a contradiction to the problem would restrict us to a narrow field of enquiry. Since Nicholas wet his bed every night, this conception of the unique outcome would have restricted our search to those occasions upon which he only half wet his bed, or perhaps to those occasions upon which he woke sooner following micturition. And as candidate unique outcomes, these would have been "slim reeds". While therapists might consider such achievements noteworthy, I think that we could quite safely predict that neither Nicholas nor his parents would attach very much significance to these events.

However, in working to identify contradictions to the dominant plot, rather than seeking contradictions to the problem, we find a broad field of enquiry opening before us. In stepping into this field, Nicholas, his parents and I, discovered an abundance of contradictions to the dominant plot of "incompetence".

Our enquiry established the following points:

1. In recent times, Nicholas had taken some steps to reduce some of the trouble he had been getting into in various places. Getting more in touch with what was in his best interests had provided the initiative for these steps.

2. In the past year, Nicholas had succeeded in challenging some very "young" habits that had been interfering with his ability to take responsibility for his behaviour. He had achieved this by getting clearer about his goals for his life, and by developing skills in advising himself.

3. Over the weeks leading up to our appointment, there had been some evidence that Nicholas had been breaking with "forgetfulness", and had begun to fine-tune his memory.

4. There had been some new developments in class at school. Instead of getting stressed out about his work, which was a feature of the past, Nicholas had developed the ability to intervene when he felt tension coming on. This intervention took the form of leaning back in his chair, putting his hands behind his head, and stretching.

5. When reviewing these developments in his life, it occurred to Mr Harris that Nicholas might have been thinking differently about things. Nicholas confirmed this speculation, saying that he had been asking himself more sensible questions.

6. Towards the end of our meeting, our discussion was focused on developing a more thorough understanding of how Nicholas had achieved these steps, and about what these steps reflected about what he wanted for his life and about this personal qualities. At a certain point in this discussion, Mr and Mrs Harris talked about how imaginative Nicholas was, and suggested that perhaps he had now managed to get his imagination working for him, rather than against him. Nicholas confirmed this.

Everybody agreed that these developments reflected competence rather than incompetence. I openly wondered about what a *competent* approach to the bed-wetting problem might look like, and then suggested that it could be a good idea for Nicholas to translate his own knowledgeableness about this into a program for dealing with this problem. He could do this by simply working out translations of the points that I had recorded during the conversation. Nicholas was enthusiastic to do this, and I am here including a copy of the document that was the outcome of these translations.

Nicholas's Escape From Bed Wetting[2]

1. *Tell myself, "I don't like having a wet bed because I would like to wake up dry. This would let me sleep in longer, feeling more comfortable and warm."*

2. *Advise myself, " I know I have to stop. This will give me more independence".*

3. *Think about how it is possible for me to remind myself to stop, even if I am asleep.*

4. *I'll go to sleep with my hands behind my head so that I don't worry so much.*

5. *I will ask myself a sensible question like, "Have I gone to the toilet?", or, "How am I going to feel when I am dry?"*

6. *Imagine how happy I will feel when I am dry.*

---

2. Permission was granted for the reproduction of the documents that appear in this paper.

Nicholas undertook to read this document to himself each night before going to sleep. And it worked. But how could this be, when it is such a simple document, and when all of the other more sophisticated and technical approaches had failed? The answer to this question is not a difficult one to arrive at. It worked because it engaged Nicholas in a consultation of his own knowledgeableness, and it served to elevate one of the counter-plots of his life - "competence".

Is it useful to supply copies of documents like this to other young people who are experiencing similar problems? Under some circumstances, and at a certain point in this work, the answer is "Yes". If these young people are having difficulty in translating various contradictions to the dominant plots of their lives into a program for dealing with these problems, seeing how this has been done by other children usually triggers some highly imaginative and unique ideas for their own translations.

STATEMENTS OF POSITION

Robert Jones was six years old and had a history of persistent soiling. His parents were physically and emotionally exhausted from this problem itself, and from their many attempts to deal with it. They were now concerned that, if the soiling wasn't soon resolved, this exhaustion would spread to their "good will", which was "becoming worn thin".

After getting to know Robert and his parents some, I engaged them in an externalizing conversation about the soiling. As they stepped into this conversation, for the first time Robert named the problem for what it was - "Mr Mischief". We spent some time together exploring the various ways that Mr Mischief had been interfering in the lives and in the relationships of family members. We also undertook the task of identifying "the Mr Mischief purposes and plans for Robert's life", and of exposing the tricks that Mr Mischief relied upon to put these purposes and plans into action.

Following this, I encouraged Robert and his parents to:

(a)   evaluate the various ways in which Mr Mischief had been influencing their lives and their relationships, and the various plans that Mr Mischief had for Robert's life: *Are you happy about what Mr Mischief is doing to your relationship with Robert, or are you unhappy about this? Does it make you cross that Mr Mischief is interfering in your friendships, or does this make you pleased?* etc.

(b) justify these evaluations of Mr Mischief's influence and purposes: *Why does it upset you so that Mr Mischief is wrecking your friendships?* and so on.

So often, when I meet with families and get to know something of the history of the concerns that bring them to therapy, I find that parents have an established position on these concerns, and so too have many of the other adults in children's lives. But rarely do I find that children have had the opportunity to establish their position on the concern, particularly when this concern specifically relates to their own lives. Perhaps this speaks of the ageism of our culture, but, whatever the case, this scenario so often sets a scene that incites adults to take action against children, and that either incites passivity in children, or recruits them into the view that *they* are the problem. And when children put the problem together with their identity, they invariably engage in self-destructive behaviours - so not only do parents take action against children in these circumstances, but children also take action against themselves. The two categories of questions that I have referred to here dismantle such impasses. They make it possible for many people to clarify, and for others to establish, a position in regard to problems that they and/or others have been concerned about. They also open new opportunities for people to articulate the preferred purposes of their lives. In so doing, these categories of questions also lay the foundations for collaborative work in therapy.

In response to these evaluation and justification questions, for the first time ever, Robert's parents witnessed him taking a position on Mr Mischief's activities. For the first time ever, they heard Robert articulate some preferences for how he would like his life to be. And, for the first time ever, they were all able to join each other in a mutual position on the problem of soiling - and this clearly had effects that were invigorating of them all.

It has been my experience that to open possibilities for children to establish a statement of position on problems can, of itself, be transformative of children's relationships with these problems, and, as well, transformative of the status of these problems. In view of this, I offered to work the notes of our first interview into a clear account of Robert's statement of position on Mr Mischief, using Robert's words as best I could. And I suggested that this be read aloud to Robert each day by his parents at an opportune time. Both offer and suggestion were received enthusiastically. I will include here the statement of position that I subsequently mailed to this family.

How Mr Mischief Messes Up Robert's Life

1.   *He gets me into trouble with Mum and Dad. I don't like this.*

2.   *He dirties my pants. I don't like this. This is uncomfortable.*

3.   *He makes other children want to go away from me. I am unhappy about this. This could make me lonely.*

4.   *He takes away my fun. I don't like this because I like having fun.*

5.   *He is making me less grown up. I am upset about this, because he will make me younger than my younger sisters.*

6.   *He is making me a follower. I don't like this because I would like to be a leader.*

7.   *He is stopping me from doing things. I'm cross about this, because I like doing lots of things, and I'd like to run faster.*

8.   *He is becoming a habit. I wouldn't like this because habits are hard to get away from. I wouldn't want a habit to rule my life.*

9.   *He could make me into a slave. I wouldn't want this, because I want better things for my life.*

10. *He is starting to make the decisions in my life. I'm not happy about this because I should be making more decisions in my life.*

I would like to get my life back from Mr Mischief. It is my life, it belongs to me. It will be difficult, but I know how to do difficult things. When I was learning to ride a bike, this was difficult. But I didn't let this push me back. I kept trying and I got the hang of it. I didn't surrender and in the end I was successful. If I keep trying to get my life back from Mr Mischief, I will get the hang of it.

Robert's articulation of this statement of position, and the acknowledgement of this by others, constituted the turning point in our work together. At the second interview, I discovered that the soiling had decreased by 50 per cent, and was no longer a daily occurrence. I also learned that,for the very first time in his life, on the occasions upon which Robert had soiled his pants, he was acknowledging this to others instead of denying it. Of course, this wasn't the end of the story, because, as one might expect, Mr Mischief turned out to be a very slippery character. I met with this family on several more occasions, identifying the skills that Robert was using to out-trick Mr Mischief, and those aspects of the parent-child team work that seemed to be working best. Before long, Robert had sealed Mr Mischief's fate - and it was apparent that Mr Mischief had become resigned to this - and he received a Certificate of Achievement.

THERAPEUTIC DOCUMENTS CHECKLIST

Given the number of demands on most people's lives in this modern world, there is always a possibility that responding to the events of daily life will take precedence over attending to correspondence arising out of the therapeutic encounter. When this happens, therapists are confronted with the "hallstand drawer" phenomenon referred to earlier in this essay, and, needless to say, this is hardly morale boosting for any of the parties to the therapeutic interaction. Because of this, it makes a great deal of sense for therapists to attend to the "receiving context" of. therapeutic documents. Attention to this receiving context will mitigate the hallstand drawer phenomenon, and will contribute greatly to people's experience of the significance of therapeutic documents. Under these circumstances, it will only be on very rare occasions that people do not consult therapeutic documents between appointments, and this usually will have to do with extenuating circumstances.

I will here provide a checklist that will assist therapists to attend to the receiving context of therapeutic documents. Although the points that I make here may seem rather extensive, it rarely takes more than five to ten minutes to work through them with family members. I do not intend for this to be an exhaustive account of the possibilities for attending to this receiving context, and it is my hope that readers will experiment with these ideas, and perhaps add to, subtract from, and/or derive modifications of them, according to the feedback they receive from the people who consult them.

As therapists become more experienced in trafficking in therapeutic documents, they may find that a specific focus on the preparation of the receiving context becomes less necessary - that many elements of their ongoing work are referenced to this issue.

1. Introduction to Therapeutic Documents

(a)   The therapist introduces the idea of constructing a therapeutic document, talks about how this might be appropriate to the circumstances at hand, and gives some account of how such documents have been useful to other people under similar circumstances (if the people who are consulting the therapist are of oral culture, or if they are not literate, then audiotapes can substitute for written documents).

(b)   The therapist shares his/her thoughts about the sorts of issues that such a document might address, all the while taking care not to impose the idea - people need to be assured that such documents are in no way essential to this work. At this time, the question is posed: "Would you interested in receiving such a document?"

(c) If people have some enthusiasm to proceed with this, the therapist introduces a discussion about the form that it might be appropriate for the document to take - a standard letter, a charter, a statement of position, a letter of reference, a document of identity, etc.

(d) When a decision has been reached about form, the therapist can engage people in a discussion about the processes of preparation of the document. For example, is this something over which everybody concerned should collaborate, or is there some preference for the therapist to prepare this after the session from her/his notes?

2. Delivery, Circulation, and Safe Keeping

(a) If the document is to be mailed or to be collected after the interview, decisions are taken about the particularities of this. This is important, for sometimes the document is to be received by a child who does not ordinarily collect the mail. At times it might go to a person who is living in a shared household, hostel, or boarding house - under these circumstances confidentiality may be an issue, and an alternative mailing address may be necessary. And at times it will go to a post office box that, in the usual run of events, is not regularly cleared.

(b) As the ready accessibility of therapeutic documents is important, the therapist can ask people what plans they might put into place to ensure that these documents will be available for them to consult whenever this is desirable. To facilitate this, at times it will be important for people to find someone to entrust their therapeutic documents to. This is particularly important for people who have no regular place of abode, or who are vulnerable to circumstances that could separate them from their therapeutic documents at the very time that they most need to consult them.

(c) Decisions can then be made about who else should read these documents, about how they might be engaged in so doing, and the circumstances of this. This is important, because many therapeutic documents are directed at recruiting an audience to the significant developments in people's lives - audiences that might provide acknowledgement of these developments, audiences that are likely to be authenticating of some of the new identity claims that are reflected in the documents.

(d) A decision is then taken as to how many copies of the document will be required.

3. Circumstances of Consultation and Making Predictions

(a) At this point, discussion focuses on the identification of the circumstances under which the document might be consulted. This might be according to some pre-established schedule, at contemplative moments, under circumstances of duress when a person is most likely to be at risk of being dispossessed of their knowledgeableness, and so on.

(b) It is now time to invite people to speculate about the consequences of consulting therapeutic documents. What effect do they imagine this consultation could have on their responses to the problematic circumstances, and on their lives and relationships more generally? People can be encouraged to render this speculation into specific predictions, which can be included in the documents, or perhaps recorded separately, and then sealed in an envelope and filed away until the next session.

The therapist makes it clear that these predictions are not being taken as a commitment to action, but that it will nonetheless be interesting to find out how accurate people can be in making these. When predictions are recorded separately and sealed in an envelope, this can be opened at the next meeting, and checked against developments.

4.   **Review of Prediction**

(a)   At the next interview, the events that took place between sessions are reviewed to identify those circumstances that warranted a consultation of therapeutic documents. People's predictions about the effects of these consultations are checked against subsequent events.

(b)   If this review verifies people's predictions, then the therapist can invite them to reflect on the significance of the accuracy of these predictions. The usual outcome of this reflection is that people acknowledge the extent to which they are becoming "authorities" on their own lives. A discussion about what this might mean about their ability to influence the shape of their lives can then be initiated, followed by some explorations about what this might suggest about possibilities for future steps.

(c)   If a review of events contradicts people's predictions, then the therapist can initiate an investigation into what vital pieces of information may have been missing from the documents, and/or can again take the people who are consulting them through points 1, 2 & 3 of this checklist, this time paying closer attention to detail. In doing so, the therapeutic documents and the receiving context of these documents might be revised in ways that will make it more possible for them to have the desired effects on future occasions.

CONCLUSION

The therapeutic practices of the written word that I describe in this paper are time-efficient and do not require specific writing skills on the part of the therapist. Nonetheless, they can make a profound contribution to the therapeutic endeavour. I would encourage readers to explore the construction of documents of this sort with the people who consult them, and to refer to the therapeutic documents checklist when preparing a receiving context for these documents. I have no doubt that all parties to the therapeutic interaction will find their efforts amply rewarded.

9. Behaviour and its Determinants or Action and its Sense: Systems & Narrative Metaphors

The narrative metaphor is often referred to in conjunction with other metaphors that are commonly used in family therapy literature and practice: specifically, metaphors of system and pattern. It is very often assumed that the narrative metaphor can be tacked on to these other metaphors, and the narrative metaphor is often conflated with them. Because the metaphors of system and pattern on the one hand, and the metaphor of narrative on the other, are located in distinct and different traditions of thought, this tacking on and conflation of disparate metaphors simply does not work, and, in my view, suggests a lack of awareness of the basic premises and the very different political consequences that are associated with these different metaphors.

Let me first briefly review some important implications of the metaphors of system and of pattern:

1. When we say that behaviour is functional, that it is rule-governed, that it serves purposes related to the maintenance of equilibrium or homeostasis, or whatever, and that behaviour is patterned, we are engaging in the thoroughly institutionalised and time-honored practice of connecting behaviour to its determinants.

2. In that the metaphor of system relates to theories of equilibrium, of the maintenance of order, of stability and so on, and in that the metaphor of pattern relates to theories of regularity or of redundancy, both metaphors construct a timeless reality. The metaphor of system introduces the notion that there exist relatively independent entities called systems that stand outside of, or survive apart from, the ravages of time. And since the criterion for verifying a pattern is the identification of a redundancy across time, then immunity or invulnerability to the effects of time is built into its very definition.

3. The metaphors of system and pattern encourage therapists to assume objectivity, and to step into a formal vocabulary of language that emphasises a posture of spectatorship and impartiality.

However, when we challenge the time-honored practice of connecting behaviour to its determinants, when "explanation comes to be regarded as a matter of connecting action to its sense rather than behaviour to its determinants", the metaphors of system and of pattern do not "prosper" - they evaporate. Here I am using the words of anthropologist Clifford Geertz, and perhaps I should cite the whole of his celebrated quote on the subject of the refiguration of social theory:

> ... a challenge is being mounted to some of the central assumptions of mainstream social science. The strict separation of theory and data, the "brute fact" idea; the effort to create a formal vocabulary of analysis purged of all subjective reference, the "ideal language" idea; and the claim to moral neutrality and the Olympian view, "the God's truth" idea - none of these can prosper when explanation comes to be regarded as a matter of connecting action to its sense rather than behaviour to its determinants. The refiguration of social theory represents, or will if it continues, a sea change in our notion not so much of what knowledge is but of what it is we want to know. (1983, p.34)

And when explanation comes to be regarded as a matter of connecting action to its sense, we are introduced to the world of interpretation, and to the world of narrative. I will now contrast those implications of the metaphors of system and pattern with some of the implications of the metaphor of narrative:

1. When we break from the time-honored notion of connecting behaviour to its determinants through the construction of formal systems of analysis that prove what did happen is what had to happen, and when instead we begin to explore the connection of action to its sense or meaning, we turn our attention to processes of interpretation; to how persons make sense of their experience, to how they endow their experiences of life with meaning. And when this happens, we find ourselves entering the territory of narrative, for when people are engaged in meaning-making they are engaged in telling stories about their own and each other's lives.

    When we connect action to its sense, we enter what I would refer to as more of a *constitutionalist* perspective on life. We attend to how persons are actively engaged in making their lives up as they go about the processes of attributing meaning to their experience, to how persons shape and re-shape their lives as they tell and re-tell, or as they perform and re-perform the stories of their lives, as they go about the visioning and revisioning of the accounts of their history and of their future.

    When we connect action to its sense, we are resurrecting and elevating the factor of consciousness in the explanation of the acts and the events of people's lives. We are encouraged to prioritise people's notions of what they are doing and why they are doing it, their views about how things came to be the way that they are, and so on. In our efforts to understand the lives of others, we find ourselves attentive to their interpretations of their actions in terms of particular accounts of desire, whim, intention, purpose, motive, ambition, goal, plan, commitment, vision and so on.

    When we connect action to its sense, we break from the received and unitary accounts of life, and, in the process of this, the politics of relationship are brought forth. The experiences of everyday life, the situations that provide the context for such experiences, the multiplicity of the interpretations of all this, most of which are informed by certain visionings or re-visionings of history - this is what becomes the focus of our attention. And in attending to all of this, and to the real effects of, or the consequences of, these interpretations of experience, we discern contestation as the condition of life - not order and equilibrium.[1] And when we discern contestation as the condition of life, the politics of inequality and marginalisation, of oppression and subjugation, of dominance and submission, of exploitation and resistance are foregrounded. The struggles around gender, class, race, ethnicity, age, and sexual orientation, demand acknowledgement.

2. Instead of constructing a timeless reality after the tradition of metaphors of system and pattern, in the tradition of the metaphor of narrative, time is of an essence; time and narrative are inseparable. To quote Paul Racouer on this:

> ... *time becomes human time to the extent that it is organized after the manner of a narrative; narrative, in turn, is meaningful to the extent that it portrays the feature of temporal experience.* (1984, p.3)

In that stories are constituted of events that are linked together in particular sequences through time and according to plot, narrative provides an account of people living their lives in the flow of time; it introduces what is at times referred to as a *processual* perspective. It is the sense of one's life unfolding through time that is embodied in narrative. Rather than providing for the illusion of timelessness through the construction of atemporal accounts of life that emphasise stability and equilibrium, narrative emphasises the changing nature of

---

1.   This is a point made well by Renato Rosaldo in **Culture & Truth: The Remaking of Social Analysis** (1993).

life as it is lived, and opens space for the appreciation of how persons go about negotiating the various contingencies, the uncertainties, and the irregularities of life.

3.   Rather than trafficking in those metaphors that encourage therapists to assume objectivity, and to step into a formal vocabulary of language that emphasises a posture of therapist spectatorship and impartiality, the metaphor of narrative emphasises the constitutive nature, or the life-shaping nature, of all interactions. This discourages us from entertaining the illusion of neutrality, and from proposing an innocent bystander status for ourselves.

The formal vocabularies of language to which I am referring act as a panacea for the concerns of therapists. As this serves to obscure, for therapists, the extent to which the problems that persons bring to therapy are mired in relational politics in practices of power, and in structures of domination, it brings with it a certain degree of comfort for therapists. In making it possible for us to define certain problems as an aberration rather than a product of our modes of life and thought, we are able to avoid facing our complicity in the maintenance of those aspects of these ways of life and thought that are constitutive of the very problems that persons bring to therapy.

Take, for example, the therapy of those men who perpetrate abuse. To see this abuse as a systems phenomenon would enable me, as a man, to obscure the link between the violence of these men and the dominant ways of being and thinking for men in this culture that valorise aggression, domination and conquest. It would enable me, as a man, to avoid confronting the ways that I might be complicit in the reproduction of these dominant ways of being and thinking. It would enable me, as a member of the class of men, to avoid facing the responsibility that I have to take action to contribute to the dismantling of men's privilege that perpetuates inequality of opportunity, to the destabilisation of the structures of oppression, and to the challenging of the various practices of power that are subjugating and marginalising of others. And it would enable me to continue to leave it to those persons in the least powerful position to raise issues of disqualification, discrimination, and so on, and to take action to end this.

However, in stepping apart from these formal systems of analysis, we are encouraged to acknowledge our complicity in the construction of the worlds that we share with others, and to assume a moral and ethical responsibility for the real effects of, or the consequences of, our interactions with those persons who seek our help. And, in that the metaphor of narrative breaks us from the assumption of objectivity and the illusion of neutrality, it encourages us to position ourselves by rendering transparent our location in the worlds of gender, race, class, ethnicity, sexual orientation, and so on. In the process of challenging the notion of the "detached observer", we face the requirement of positioning ourselves in our worlds, the requirement of rendering ourselves culturally visible.

This can be facilitated by various means, including through the soliciting of interpretations of our therapeutic interactions from persons who seek our help; by opening space for these persons to reflect on the processes of therapy and on their experience of our own personhood and on their experience of our conduct.

Such a positioning of ourselves, that renders us more culturally visible, goes some way toward both acknowledging and dismantling the hierarchies of power that feature in therapeutic interaction. Renato Rosaldo, in talking about the myth of detachment that is nurtured by middle and upper-middle class professionals, points out the extent to which this myth is maintained through a denial of the cultural and ethnic location of these professionals, and the extent to which the invisibility of their culture and ethnicity, as juxtaposed to the visibility of the culture and ethnicity of the "other", conceals their dominant class position and ensures their "unspoken monopoly on power".

Rosaldo associates this myth of detachment with the objectivist position, and contrasts this with the more culturally-visible position:

The objectivists . . . prefer to stand above the fray, where they can assume a position of omniscience, and work in the "clean" realm of detachment and ethical neutrality. To me, the attitudes embodied in their "standing above it all" range from mild condescension through active surveillance to brute domination; to them, their position is one of impartiality and their distance works in the service of objectivity. To me, one rarely studies culture from a neutral position, so analysts should be as explicit as possible about partisanship, interests, and feelings; to them, scholarship is disinterested inquiry in the service of truth and knowledge.
(1992, p.221)

CONCLUSION

It has been my intention here to challenge a prevalent blurring of important distinctions around metaphors that are commonly used in family therapy literature and practice. To achieve this, I have contrasted some of the implications of the metaphors of system and pattern, and some of the implications of the metaphor of narrative. These metaphors are located in very different traditions of thought, and have very different political consequences with regard to therapeutic interaction.

Contrary to oft-accepted opinion, I believe that attempts to put these metaphors together in ways that obscure these distinctions actually limit possibilities for thought and options for action in the therapeutic context. And, as well, this makes it virtually impossible for therapists to identify and confront some of the more significant questions about their work, and to set about addressing these questions.

REFERENCES

Geertz, C. 1983:
  Local Knowledge: Further Essays in Interpretive Anthropology.
  New York: Basic Books.
Racouer, P. 1984:
  Time and Narrative. Chicago: University of Chicago Press.
Rosaldo, R. 19932:
  Culture and Truth: The Remaking of Social Analysis. Boston:
  Beacon Press.